When Comes the Storm

by Cam Arensen

ISBN# 978-9966-757-45-6

Cover and author's photo: Esther Ruth Arensen
Cover & interior design: Blake Arensen

Scripture quotations unless otherwise indicated are from the English
Standard Version, copyright 2001 by Crossways, a publishing ministry of
Good News Publishers.

To Esther Ruth
My wife
My partner in life and ministry
My best friend

From the wind swept porch at RVA where we fell in love
to the soaring mountains of Alaska
the golden plains of Kenya
the desert sands of the Arabian Peninsula

Through good times and hard times
In health and now in sickness

You have stayed with me
through all the twists and turns of the journey
I thank you, I love you, and I dedicate this book to you

Introduction

Jesus once told the story of two men and their houses. One man built his house on rock. The other man built his house on sand. Then came the storm. Rain fell, floods came and wind blew. The house built on the rock stood firm. The house built on the sand collapsed.

It is a simple story with some obvious applications. I want to focus on two of them. First, the storm struck both houses. Nowhere in the Bible are we as Christ's followers promised that we will be immune from the storms of life. Quite the opposite, Jesus told us that "in this world you will have troubles." This book was born out of a storm that I experienced and continue to experience. Rain fell, floods came and wind blew. Storms come to us all. Everyone who reads these words can give testimony to their own storms of life.

The second application (and the reason for this book) is this: the time to prepare for the storms is before they come. Prevention is better than cure. Good preparation is less costly than rebuilding from the rubble. I have been a follower of Christ since I was a child. I was born and raised in East Africa in a missionary family. Biblical principles were instilled in me from an early age. I spent my career in Christian service as a pastor. I had the great privilege of spending hours each week studying the Scriptures in order to pass Biblical truth on to my congregation. I not only taught the truths of Scripture. I endeavored to "do them" like the man who built his house on the rock in Jesus' story (Matthew 7:24). As a result, when the latest storm entered my life, and rain fell and the floods came and the wind blew, I did not experience any sense of panic. I knew (as the psalmist says in Psalm 121:1-2) "where my help comes from." The latest storm was fierce and the winds were sometimes gale-force. But my house of faith stood firm because it was built on the rock. I was standing on solid ground. I didn't have to discover new truth in the crisis of the moment. I was able to review old, familiar truths; truths I had built my life on; truths I had preached to others. I re-examined these truths and I found them to be the solid ground I needed to weather the storm.

There are three kinds of people who will read this book. You may be in a calm and peaceful phase of life. The sky is blue and the sun is shining brightly. No dark clouds lurk on the horizon. This is an ideal time to read and stow away the truths contained in these pages. You may not need them today, but I can promise you this. Storms come into everyone's life. They will come into yours. This is the time to make sure that your house is built on rock. This is the time to make sure you are standing on solid ground.

You may belong to a second group of readers. The storm is currently raging around you. You are in crisis mode. The foundations of your life are being shaken. Will your faith stand the test? Are you standing on solid ground? If not, how can you find your way to that solid ground? It is my prayer that the truths expressed in these chapters will come to you in time so that you will be able to withstand the testing of the storm.

Or maybe you belong to the third group; you are surveying the rubble of your life. The storm came and your life (values, goals, dreams and aspirations) is lying in pieces around you. Everything (and everyone) you thought you could depend on (including yourself!) has failed you. You are facing the prospect of rebuilding your life from scratch. Will you rebuild on sand? Or will you rebuild on rock; on the eternal truths of God's Word? This book is a good place to start. There is an old saying: "The best time to plant a tree was twenty years ago. The second best time is today." It is never too late (or too early) to start building your life on the solid ground of God's truth.

Chapter One

HERE COMES THE STORM!

It was one of the longest walks of my life. The corridor of the hospital seemed endless. When I turned the corner, I saw the words I had been dreading over the door in front of me: **Oncology Department.**

It had all started innocently enough. I was walking with my wife through a mall one afternoon when I began to feel an odd pain in my left hip. It wasn't intense; just a nagging discomfort with each step. I stopped briefly and commented to Esther Ruth that I had "a hitch in my get-along." We then continued our walk. In the weeks that followed the pain did not get worse, but it did persist. I still didn't think too much about it. After all, I was about to celebrate my 65th birthday. Aches and pains come with the territory.

After several weeks with no improvement, I decided to see a doctor. This was contrary to my usual practice, but we had good insurance at the time and we were about to make a move that might disrupt our coverage. I called and scheduled an appointment with an orthopedic specialist. He listened to my symptoms and scheduled some x-rays and an MRI of the affected area. After my discussion with the doctor I left the clinic with some mild concerns. Was there a problem in my lower back? Was I developing arthritis in my hip? Would I need a hip replacement? Or would he simply prescribe exercise and physical therapy and mild pain relievers?

I went to see the doctor a few days later to get the results of the tests. It was a strange appointment. The doctor wouldn't meet my eyes. He fidgeted and rearranged papers on his desk and cleared his throat several times. When he spoke, he was vague and evasive. "I don't see something like this very often.

I think you need to see another specialist," was all he would say. This time I left the clinic puzzled and more than a little alarmed.

Still thinking the problem might relate to some kind of arthritis, I scheduled an appointment for the next day with a rheumatologist at a new hospital in town. I handed him the file with the x-ray and MRI results. He took one look at them and his face fell. "You need to see a spinal surgeon," he said. He called ahead to the Surgery Department in the same building, and I was soon seated in front of another doctor. He looked at my file. "This isn't something that needs surgery. You need to see another doctor in the department at the end of this hallway and around the corner."

And so my long walk began, ending in front of the Oncology Department. I took a deep breath and opened the door. The waiting room was empty. The receptionist smiled and said, "The doctor can see you now." This doctor looked at the MRI and nodded. "I think I know what this is, but I will need to run some tests to confirm it." I was soon lying on my side as he extracted samples of bone marrow from my hip.

I reflected on the day as I drove home. It had been a rather remarkable afternoon. I had seen three different doctors in three different departments. I had done no waiting. All three doctors had been sitting in their offices, almost as if they were waiting to see me. But the efficiency of the process almost added to my concerns. This couldn't be happening to me! I didn't have time to have cancer!

I was on the cusp of retiring from a lifetime in Christian ministry. For the last twenty-five years, I had been the pastor of an international, English-speaking church in Abu Dhabi, the capital of the United Arab Emirates. I had announced my plans to retire in November, 2015. A succession plan had been put in place. It was now the end of October. I had three more messages to preach and a flurry of farewell events before we said our final farewells and boarded the plane. Now this?

Two days later I once again sat across the desk from the same German doctor. He confirmed my worst fears. I had a form of cancer called Multiple Myeloma. As I soon found out, Multiple Myeloma is a cancer of the blood. The bone marrow starts to produce too many blood plasma cells. If unchecked, these cells migrate through the body. They can collect in soft tissue tumors, often at the base of the spine. They also infiltrate the bones and cause bone lesions and severe pain. In my case, I had a soft tissue tumor wrapped around the sciatic nerve in my left hip, as well as lesions in my lower back. The doctor tried to be encouraging and painted as rosy a picture as he could, but I left his office stunned, numb. As I shared the details with my wife, we wept together. Everything we had planned was now in question. The following Friday (our church in Abu Dhabi met on Fridays to coincide with the day off in a Muslim country) I stood in front of the congregation to share what the doctor had told me. I knew the announcement would carry significant shock value. I had been the pastor of the church for many years. For some in the congregation I was the only pastor they had ever known. As their spiritual shepherd (for a few more weeks), I wanted to minister to them and to help them process what I was going through and, if possible, turn it into a teaching opportunity.

I began my message with a question. "Is your life simple, or is it complicated?" Of course I expected that the vast majority of people in any congregation would respond that their lives were complicated. I continued:

> I know my life seemed very complicated in recent days, as we are in the final throes of our transition and departure from Abu Dhabi. We are facing all the normal decisions of packing and shipping and extracting ourselves from our life here. In addition, I've been dealing with all the challenges of remembering the details for turning over my responsibilities to new leaders. Then something happened that at first seemed to make everything immensely more complex. But at the same time, God took me back to passages of Scripture and messages I have preached in the past. God challenged me to "practice what I preach." These passages have reminded me that life is actually very simple.

Now I recognize that I may seem to be speaking in riddles, so let me explain myself.

I then shared with the congregation the events of the previous weeks, culminating in the news of my cancer diagnosis. My throat tightened. I choked up a few times as I talked. When I uttered the word "cancer" there was an audible gasp from the congregation followed by an intense silence. Many had tears in their eyes.

What Scripture passages did I use to minister to God's people that day? And how did these Scriptures remind me that life (in spite of its complexities) was really, in its fundamentals, still very simple?

The first passage I used comes from Philippians chapter 1. When Paul wrote the book of Philippians, his life was more than a little complicated. He was in prison in Rome. He was awaiting trial. He did not know if he would be released or condemned and executed. That sounds complicated! But as we read the letter we find that for Paul, life was simple. Oh, the details were complicated, but Paul had the big picture well and truly focused. And that big picture was really very simple.

Paul expresses this clearly by boiling life down to its most basic components in Philippians 1:21:

For to me to live is Christ, and to die is gain.

For Paul, life was simple because he knew the answer to two basic questions. The first is: **What is my life for?** The second question is: **What comes after?** If we have a clear answer to those two questions, then suddenly life becomes very simple.

What is my life for?
Paul's answer to that question is found in the first half of the verse. "For to me to live is Christ." For Paul, life was all about Christ. From the life-changing day on the road to Damascus when he was confronted by the risen Christ, Jesus was front and center in his life. All else was secondary. Knowing Christ, walking with him, loving him, obeying him, serving him.

"For to me to live is Christ." No matter what life dished up, that didn't change for Paul. There is an expansion of what Paul means when he says in verse 20, "As it is my eager expectation and hope that I will not be ashamed, but that with full courage now as always Christ will be honored in my body, whether by life or by death."

The word "honored" means to magnify or to make large. That is what life was for, for Paul. And, as I shared with the congregation that day, that is what my life is for. It is "for Christ." It is to honor him and to make him large; to exalt him and to cause him to be honored and praised. That has been my desire since I gave my life to Christ as young boy. It has been my desire during more than forty years of pastoral ministry on three different continents. Cancer and retirement can't change that. To honor Christ in my body and as long as I live in this body; to bring him honor by serving him and displaying his character in my attitudes, words, actions and relationships. That is my eager expectation and my hope; that my faith will not fail now, but that "with full courage" Christ will be honored in my body, "whether by life or by death."

That brings us to the second half of the verse and the second "simplifying" question: **What comes after?** Here again, Paul had a very simple and clear answer:

For to me to live is Christ **and to die is gain** (Philippians 1:21).

Paul expounds on what he means by this in the following verses:

> [22] If I am to live in the flesh, that means fruitful labor for me. Yet which I shall choose I cannot tell. [23] I am hard pressed between the two. My desire is to depart and be with Christ, for that is far better (Philippians 1: 22-23).

Paul did not fear death. In fact he looked forward to it. These verses describe the Christian view of death and eternity in a nutshell. For the follower of Christ, "to die is gain." It means to "depart and be with Christ." Death is a departure, a leaving. But for Christ's followers, it is also a destination: "To be with Christ, for that is far better."

It is often said that, "You are not really ready to live until you are ready to die." Can we truly answer the question, "What is life for?" and give ourselves wholeheartedly to the answer for that question until we know and have full confidence to the answer to the question: "What comes after?" Surely the answers to these two questions will be intricately entwined in our hearts, minds and emotions. Only when we are confident of what comes after death will we be free to truly invest our lives in the things which really matter. With the cloud of cancer hanging over my head, my life span may be shorter than I originally anticipated. But I still know what my remaining life (whatever its length) is for.

During my life and years of ministry, when facing conflict situations, I have found myself looking for win-win solutions. I was not always successful in that search, but in facing my cancer I found in Paul's words the ultimate win-win scenario. If I live (and as long as I live) I have a positive, life-affirming reason for living: to serve Christ and lift him up. If I die (when I die) – that is even better. I win either way!

Richard Baxter, the great 17th century Puritan church leader, captures the simplicity of this win-win scenario in this poem:

> *"Lord, it belongs not to my care*
> *Whether I die or live.*
> *To love and serve thee is my share*
> *And this thy grace must give.*
> *If life be long I will be glad*
> *That I may long obey.*
> *If short, then why should I be sad*
> *To rise to endless day?"*

There were additional Scriptures that I shared with the people that day: some from the Old Testament and some from the New, yet they echo and reinforce the same basic message.

As I had thought back and meditated on them, they also had the effect of calming my fears and making life simple.

The first Old Testament passage is Proverbs 3:5-6:

> Trust in the Lord with all your heart, and do not lean on your own understanding. In all your ways acknowledge him, and he will make straight your paths.

This is what I said to the congregation that day:

> I have a favorite coffee mug, given to me by a good friend. On one side it has just a single word: **TRUST**. On the other side is the verse Psalm 91:2: "God is my refuge and my fortress, my God in whom I trust." I have often found myself reaching for this mug when I faced a particularly challenging day at work. In the days since my cancer diagnosis, I have been reaching for it every morning. The word "trust" can be both a noun and a verb. In Proverbs 3:5, it is a verb and it is in the imperative, command form. The Hebrew word for trust carries in it the idea of placing complete confidence in something – enough to lean or put your weight down on it. One commentator gives the meaning, "to hang confidently." The picture the word brings to my mind is that of a rock climber working his way up a sheer cliff. Carefully he establishes and tests each handhold or foothold. But to advance up the face of the cliff, there comes the moment when he must let go of his previous, secure handhold and "hang confidently" on the next one. He must "trust" that it will hold his weight. "Trust in the Lord with all your heart," we are told. That is the hard part, is it not? We want to lean on our own understanding and to figure things out for ourselves. But God commands us: "Trust me."
>
> What is the result of this kind of trust in God? A second Old Testament passage gives the answer, found in Isaiah 26:3-4. It reads this way in the New International Version:
>
> ³ You will keep in perfect peace him whose mind is

steadfast, because he trusts in you. [4] Trust in the Lord forever, for the Lord, the Lord is the Rock eternal.

The word for peace in that verse is the Hebrew word, "shalom." Shalom and its related words are among the most important theological words in the Old Testament. It is most commonly translated "peace" in the English translations, but it means more than the absence of conflict. Completeness, wholeness, harmony, fulfillment and deep contentment are all included in this word. The translation "perfect peace" is a valiant effort to render a Hebrew idiom into English. What the Hebrew text actually does is simply repeat the word "shalom" twice for special emphasis. "You will keep in peace, peace the one whose mind is steadfast because he trusts in you." Peace, peace. Peace squared. Perfect peace. Peace in the face of cancer. Peace in the face of all of life's difficulties. Isaiah is addressing God himself. "You, God, will keep him in perfect peace…" God himself promises to protect us and keep us in a state of perfect peace when our minds are steadfast because we trust (hang confidently) in him.

So how do we hang confidently on Yahweh? How do we arrive at this place of trust, and how is this trust expressed? For the answer to this question, we turn to the New Testament, once again to Paul's letter to the Philippians. In Philippians 4:6-7 we read:

[6] Do not be anxious about anything, but in everything by prayer and supplication with thanksgiving let your requests be made known to God. [7] And the peace of God, which surpasses all understanding, will guard your hearts and minds in Christ Jesus.

We express our trust through prayer. These verses offer a happy exchange. When we turn our anxieties into prayers, God takes our prayers and gives us his peace. What's more, it is a peace that passes understanding. It is a peace that makes no sense to the natural man. It is a peace that we experience not because of circumstances, but oftentimes in spite of them. It is peace in the face of cancer.

Yes, during the last few days since my cancer diagnosis, in many ways life has become very complicated. But in a very deep and fundamental way, it has also become very simple. It became simple because I know the answer to the two key questions: What is life for? What comes after? And because I have put my trust in my wise, powerful and loving heavenly Father. He knows exactly what he is doing and why he is doing it. I don't have to figure it all out. All I have to do is trust him. Trust keeps life simple.

I closed my message to the congregation that day in October, 2015, by asking them to pray for me. I gave them a specific prayer I wanted them to take to the Father on my behalf. It was based on Paul's words in Philippians 1:20:

As it is my eager expectation and my hope that I will not be at all ashamed, but that with full courage now as always Christ will be honored in my body, whether by life or by death.

I paraphrased it this way: "Pray that God will give me the degree of health and length of life that will enable me to bring the greatest honor to the name of Jesus."

Simple? Yes. But nobody said it was easy!

Chapter Two

FOLLOW ME!

To begin this chapter, I need to go back in time, just prior to my cancer diagnosis. While I was already struggling with the pain in my hip, I had not yet seen the doctor. I had no idea how my life was about to be turned upside down. I was preaching a message from John 21 in preparation for a baptism service we would be having two weeks later. The theme of the message was this: **If we believe, we must follow.** If we truly believe in Jesus and his claims, then we must truly follow him on the path of discipleship and obedience. In the chapter, Peter and six of his fellow disciples decide to go fishing. We don't know if they intended it to be a permanent return to their former careers, or just a temporary respite from the intensity of all that had happened in the turbulence of the previous few weeks. In any case, Jesus appeared to them on the shore to call them back to their commitment to follow him.

In the story, Jesus particularly focuses on Peter. In an act of great grace and love, he publicly restores Peter and commissions him in the presence of the other disciples. I won't go through all the points in that sermon, but I do want to highlight the final one. In the account, after Peter has three times indicated his love for the Lord, Jesus makes this prophecy in John 21:18-19:

> [18] Truly, truly, I say to you, when you were young, you used to dress yourself and walk wherever you wanted, but when you are old, you will stretch out your hands and another will dress you and carry you where you do not want to go. [19] (This he said to show by what kind of death he was to glorify God). And after saying this he said to him, 'Follow me.'

With these sobering words ringing in his ears, Peter did

something very, very human. He turned and saw John following them, and he asked, "Lord, what about this man?" We are all curious. We all love to compare. I grew up with four brothers. We were always at it. Who got the biggest piece of cake? Who had the most difficult chores to complete on Saturday? Why me (or why not me)? What about him? Jesus answers Peter sternly in verse 22:

> If it is my will that he remain until I come, what is that to you? You follow me!

The point I made in my sermon from this exchange is this: **Following Jesus is an unconditional and personal act of submission to the unique path he has chosen for me.**

The word order in the original Greek text is very powerful and instructive. **You** (second person singular pronoun) **Me** (first person singular pronoun) **Follow** (second person singular imperative). It is a command and it is personal. "Peter, this isn't about John or anyone else. This is between you and me. YOU! ME! FOLLOW!

So, why am I sharing this segment of my sermon? As I was preaching this final point that day it was as though the Holy Spirit nudged me sharply and whispered in my ear, "Pay attention! This one's for you. You're going to need this." I have often been convicted in my own study and by my own preaching. But this was different. This was much stronger and more specific and personal. It was not an audible voice, but it seemed almost as clear. I didn't know what to make of it at the time, but it remained in the back of my mind. In less than a week I was sitting across the desk from the doctor as he told me I had cancer. Jesus' words came back to me. Was this the unique path he had chosen for me?

Just a few weeks after that, I was flat on my back in the hospital. The pain was so intense I could not get in or out of bed without help. When they came to get me for radiation treatments, they brought a gurney and two orderlies would pick me up and slide me from my bed onto the gurney. As they did, Jesus' words to Peter came to mind:

When you were young, you used to dress yourself and walk wherever you wanted, but when you are old, you will stretch out your hands and another will dress you and carry you where you do not want to go (John 21:18).

As they wheeled me through the halls of the hospital, I lay there helplessly looking up and seeing signs to places I didn't want to go: surgery, dirty laundry, radiation.

Was this the path God had chosen? And if so, was I willing to submit to his will? Was I ready to trust him? Was I willing to follow him in obedience on this unique path? It was not one I would have chosen for myself, but a path that he chose for me – and one that could lead to God's glory if I would remain faithful.

I had time to wrestle with those questions during those days in the hospital. As I did, God reminded me of another portion of Scripture that he had used to minister to me in previous times of crisis. It is found in Ecclesiastes 7:13-14:

> [13] Consider the work of God: who can make straight what he has made crooked? [14] In the day of prosperity be joyful, and in the day of adversity consider: God has made the one as well as the other, so that man may not find out anything that will be after him.

When I sat across the desk from the doctor in late October and he told me I had cancer, my life got bent. And I couldn't straighten it! It was a life-altering moment. I was on one path, pursuing one plan, when suddenly, without warning everything changed, and I was on another path, facing an uncertain and frightening set of challenges and circumstances. It was what the writer of Ecclesiastes refers to as a "day of adversity."

We all have them; these days of adversity. They vary from the petty and temporary annoyances of life to the life-shattering, life-altering, "nothing will ever be the same again" days; days when what is bent cannot be straightened. In these days of adversity, the writer invites us to consider and contemplate the sovereignty of God. Every day that comes into our lives and every circumstance we face comes to us within the sovereign plan and purpose of God. "Consider the work of God," we are commanded. This is no accident or random circumstance that I was facing. This was a work of God. The next verse spells it out even more clearly.

In the day of prosperity be joyful, and in the day of adversity consider, God has made the one as well as the other...

The first part of that verse is easy to obey. "In the day of prosperity be joyful." By God's grace we do experience many days of prosperity. We should relish and enjoy those days and be joyful, receiving them as precious gifts from our heavenly Father. The second part is where the challenge comes. "In the day of adversity, consider: God has made the one as well as the other."

I am not wise enough to resolve the ancient paradoxes of suffering and pain; whether God causes them or permits them; how this all relates to Satan and his attacks on God's people; where the discipline of the Lord may or may not fit into the picture. The subject is too big and complex. But I do want to affirm this clear declaration of this Scripture – that "days of adversity" are part of the sovereign plan of God. This was a reality that I had to come to grips with if I was to respond correctly to the "bending" of my life.

When we consider this reality, what do we discover? The verse ends, "so that man may not find out anything that will be after him." We discover that God is still God and we are not. That is the fundamental reality of the universe. God is God. We are not. He is sovereign. We are not. We can plan and work and arrange things as much as we like, and at the end of the day, God is in control. We can only live one day at a time because we do not know what the next day will bring. If it brings prosperity, we will rejoice. If it brings adversity (cancer!) I must still recognize that God is sovereign over all things. And in that recognition comes the challenge. Can I still trust him? Will I still follow him on the unique path of discipleship he has chosen for me?

We examined the importance of trust in the previous chapter. As I struggled with my own days of pain in the hospital, God reminded me of another word, also in the form of a command. It is a kind of corollary to the word "trust." The word is "wait." Trust alone may sometimes seem to slip into a kind of passive resignation. But waiting, along with trust, keeps hope alive. It is waiting with the confidence that God has a good purpose in mind, and it is a good purpose in this life as well as in eternity.

The Psalms are full of the command to wait. One of my favorites is Psalm 27:13-14:

> [13] I believe that I shall look upon the goodness of the Lord in the land of the living! [14] Wait for the Lord; be strong and let your heart take courage; wait for the Lord!

As I lay on my hospital bed, I did not know what the future held. I did not know "what would come after." As I write this chapter more than two years later, I still don't. But I know that God is still God and I am not. And that's OK, because I trust in God, and in trust, I am willing to wait.

In the days after I revealed my cancer diagnosis to the congregation, there was a great outpouring of prayer for me. I will always be grateful for each and every one who prayed. Many shared with me (in person and by phone messages and e-mail) that they were praying for my complete healing. I was grateful for those prayers as well. Believe me, I was praying the same thing! But the next time I was well enough to stand in the pulpit again, I shared with the congregation this word of testimony. **I believe in miracles. But I trust in God.**

In other words, I firmly believe in miracles and in the sovereign power of God which is his to display whenever and wherever it suits his purpose. But much deeper than my belief in miracles is my trust in God and in his wisdom and love and compassion and mercy and in his plan to display his glory.

And so I trust. And so I wait. And, yes, so I will follow Christ on the unique path of discipleship he has chosen for me, so that he may be glorified whether by the manner of my living or by the manner of my dying.

Chapter Three

WALKING THROUGH THE VALLEY

During my time in the hospital I had time to reflect and pray. As I did, God began to recall to my mind different sermons I had preached. It was almost as if God was continuing to challenge me. "Do you really believe what you say you believe? Are you ready to practice what you preach?" It is easy to answer a glib "Yes" to such a question. But to answer honestly, I had to examine my heart and my teaching more deeply. I had to go back to those messages and those passages of Scripture to see if they provided the answers and the confidence and strength that I needed to face my new reality. So I went back and listened to my own messages and allowed God's Word to minister to me in very deep and personal ways. And yes, I found God's presence and God's truth to be sufficient for my needs in those difficult days and to give me a strong foundation to face whatever may lie ahead. I was standing on solid ground.

The purpose of the rest of this book is to examine some of those Scripture passages and sermons, and to reproduce them in a written form, with the hope and prayer that God may use them to minister to others who are passing through the deep waters of personal illness, suffering or crisis.

One passage of Scripture came to me repeatedly when I was in the hospital. It is one of the best known and best loved passages in the Bible: Psalm 23, often referred to as the Shepherd's Psalm.

The authorship is attributed to King David, as he reflected on his years as a shepherd in the hills above Bethlehem, tending his father's sheep. Borrowing on that experience, he uses the image of the shepherd to depict his relationship with God. He begins the psalm with the remarkable words, "The Lord is my shepherd."

The whole psalm is filled with encouraging truths for the believer, but I found one particular sentence of particular comfort during the sleepless nights in the hospital. Because I memorized the psalm as child in the old King James Version, these are the words that came back to comfort me.

Yea, though I walk through the valley of the shadow of death, I will fear no evil for thou art with me (Psalm 23:4a).

What image comes into your mind when you hear the word "valley"? Most of us are conditioned by the valleys we have experienced where we live and on our travels. Often these may have been broad, gently sloping expanses. I grew up on the edge of the Rift Valley in Kenya. In front of our home on the escarpment, it was over 80 miles wide. We could barely even see the other side.

However, in trying to put ourselves in David's sandals, we have to put such pictures out of our minds. David's choice of word for valley in Psalm 23 is more akin to the Middle Eastern term "wadi"; a steep-sided ravine, cut by the erosion of seasonal rainfall and occasional flooding. As David led his sheep through the hills seeking the next watering hole or grazing spot, it was often necessary to pass through these wadis or steep-sided valleys. In the dazzle of sunlight reflecting off the rocks and cliffs all around, such valleys were often marked by dark shadows, looking pitch black to the undilated eye still squinting in the sun's bright glare. It was not uncommon for the sheep to shy away from entering such shadowy depths. It was difficult to see into the valley, to see where the chasms and crevasses might lie. Such valleys also held a host of hiding places for potential predators. It took all of the shepherd's skill to gently persuade his sheep to go with him into the valley. This is the real life picture that David drew on as he wrote the 4th verse of Psalm 23.

It is this particular verse that has made this psalm such a common choice for recitation at funerals and memorial services. Certainly that application to death's dark valley was much on my mind as I considered my cancer and the possible nearing approach of my own death. However, it is interesting to look more closely at the background and use of this word, because the phrase "shadow of death" is a single word in the Hebrew text. While it can be literally rendered "death-shadow", the word is often used in contexts where physical death is clearly not in view. In such cases it is often used with parallel words which emphasize darkness and gloom. My edition of the New International Version even puts in the footnote the alternative translation, "the darkest valley." Another way of rendering it might be, "through the valley of deepest shadow."

This should not rob this verse of its comfort in the face of death, but rather expand its comfort to other difficult times in our lives. Surely facing death, either our own or that of someone near and dear to us, is one of the deepest, darkest valleys we may face. But it is not the only valley we will traverse on our journey through life. I believe the truths of this verse are applicable to all the valleys, all the dark and scary and painful times in our lives.

Yea, though I walk through the valley of deepest shadow.

I wonder what was in David's mind when he penned those words. David had his share of valley experiences to choose from, didn't he? There was the day King Saul grabbed his spear and threw it, trying to nail David to the wall. He spent years fleeing like a common fugitive from Saul. Then there was the day he heard that all the priests at the tabernacle, who had given him bread to eat, had been slaughtered for helping him. One day he and his men came back from battle and found their village burned and all their families taken captive. His men blamed David for it and even talked of stoning him. Does that sound like a valley to you? What about the day the message came that his best friend Jonathan was dead, slain in battle by the Philistines? Or what about that painful time in David's life, when his son Absalom tried to overthrow him in a coup and David had to flee for his life? The report of the battle came back. David's forces had carried the battle, but his son Absalom was dead. David wept bitterly: "O Absalom, my son, my son! If only I had died instead of you – O Absalom, my son!" (2 Samuel 18:33).

Oh, yes, David walked through his share of dark, shadowed valleys. I'd passed through my own dark valleys in life. Now I was passing through another one, darker and more threatening than any I had experienced before. And here, once again, were these reassuring words:

> Yea, though I walk through the valley of deepest shadow, I will fear no evil.

What does David mean? Does he mean that nothing bad will ever happen to him? Obviously that would be absurd, based on the list of David's true life experiences that we have just mentioned. Clearly David does not mean that there won't be scary times, dark times, painful times in our lives. What he does mean is that we don't have to be afraid of those times or be afraid in those times.

How can that be? How can we go through those dark valleys of life without being afraid? It is the next phrase that gives the answer, and this is the answer that I kept coming back to in my own dark valley: "For thou art with me."

This is the key to facing life's valleys without that soul-paralyzing fear; without that awful sense of despair or that terrible sense of loneliness and abandonment that fear brings. "God, you are with me. I am not alone." This has been the comforting promise of God to his people down through the ages: "I will be with you." It is truly amazing how consistently this note resonates through the Scriptures.

Maybe you recall the story of Jacob in Genesis 28. He was running away, fleeing for his life. As he left his father's home, leaving all that was familiar behind, God appeared to him in a dream. What was God's great promise to Jacob? It is found in Genesis 28:15:

> I am with you and will watch over you wherever you go,

and I will bring you back to this land. I will not leave you...

What about the story of Moses? God appeared to him in the burning bush and commissioned him to go to Egypt and lead the nation of Israel to freedom. Moses was afraid. I would have been afraid too. What did God promise him? Look at Exodus 3:12:

And God said, "I will be with you."

How about Joshua? After forty years of ministering in Moses' shadow as his second in command, the day came when Moses died. The whole weight of leadership now rested on Joshua's shoulders; not just leadership but the responsibility of conquest. He was commissioned to lead the people into the Promised Land. He was afraid. How did God reassure him? Look at Joshua 1:9:

Have I not commanded you? Be strong and courageous. Do not be terrified; do not be discouraged, for the Lord your God will be with you wherever you go.

Then there was Jeremiah. God gave Jeremiah one of the toughest assignments in the Bible. He told him to go and tell the nation of Judah that God was going to punish them and send them into captivity. It was a painful and unpopular message, and the people were going to hate him for preaching it. Jeremiah didn't want the assignment. I wouldn't have wanted the assignment either. But look how God reassured him in Jeremiah 1:7-8:

7 But the Lord said to me, "Do not say, 'I am only a child.' You must go to everyone I send you to and say whatever I command you. 8 Do not be afraid of them, for I am with you and will rescue you," declares the Lord.

Are you starting to see the pattern here? God doesn't promise us an easy path. He doesn't promise us that there will be no danger. He doesn't promise that there will be no pain. But he does promise us this: *I will be with you.*

This is the promise of the Shepherd to the sheep as he leads them into the valley. And David, as one of God's sheep, takes this comfort to heart.

Yea though I walk through the valley of deepest shadow,
I will fear no evil for Thou art with me.

When I was about seven years old, my Dad took me on a hippo hunt. We were living on the edge of Lake Victoria in Tanzania, and occasionally when a large church conference was planned, Dad would shoot a hippo. It was a great way to feed a large number of people. One day he took me along.

I was excited as we climbed into the African canoe. My father and I sat in the middle and several Tanzanian men sat in the front and back to paddle. We paddled out to where a herd of hippos was floating in the lake. All we could see were their eyes and nostrils above the surface of the water. The men paddled the boat as close as they could. When one of the hippos surfaced within range, Dad took quick and careful aim and squeezed the trigger, "Boom!"

The hippo sank from sight, leaving a dark trail of blood. Normally with a brain shot, the hippo dies instantly and sinks. All that remains is to wait for the carcass to float, pull it to shore and then butcher it. But that day, Dad's shot must have been a little off target. Suddenly, about 10 feet away, the hippo came roaring up almost entirely out of the water with his jaws wide open! With a tremendous splash, he fell back into the water and disappeared again. A few seconds later, he came rearing up out of the water a second time! Again he fell back with a great splash. I was gripping the edge of the boat. I thought, "What if he comes up under the boat next time?" The hippo made a couple more desperate plunges before he sank for the last time. That day is still vivid in my mind. I remember being excited, even nervous. But I also remember that on another, much deeper level, I was not afraid. Do you know why? Because my Dad was in the boat with me. I had total trust that my father would not allow me to come to any harm. With him near, I was safe.

I must confess to you that I have since thought back on that experience from an adult's perspective. It has occurred to me that if that hippo had decided to attack our boat, there probably wasn't much my father could have done about it. I grew up thinking of hippos as relatively benign, but I have since read that they are responsible for more deaths in Africa than any other wild animal. I have come to realize that there was real danger that day, and a part of me now wants to shout, "Dad, what were you thinking?!?!? We could have been killed!"

But here is the difference. In the boat that day, I felt safe because I had absolute trust in my father, and I knew he was with me. I realize now that my father was not omnipotent and that there were limits to his protection. But my heavenly Father *is* omnipotent. He has no limits and there are no limits to his protection.

The essence of the Good Shepherd's protection is his presence. He doesn't promise that nothing bad will ever happen. He does promise that, no matter how dark the valley, he will walk through it with us. He promises his presence.

I sensed his presence in the hospital during the long nights. I have sensed it since, during the phases of treatment and the ups and downs that every cancer patient experiences. When I haven't sensed it, I have gone back to this verse and its promise and laid hold of it by faith, clinging to it like a drowning man to a lifeline. As I write these words, my health is stable and my immediate prognosis is good. But I know that, sooner or later, apart from divine intervention, this cancer will return, and I will again enter the dark valley. But I am not afraid, for I know that I will not enter the valley alone. My Shepherd will go with me.

God often used Christian music to encourage me during the darkest days of my illness. One particular song was especially powerful. Written and sung by Lynda Randle, the words go like this:

Life is easy, when you're up on the mountain
And you've got peace of mind, like you've never known
But things change, when you're down in the valley
Don't lose faith, for you're never alone
For the God on the mountain, is the God in the valley
When things go wrong, He'll make them right
And the God of the good times
Is still God in the bad times
The God of the day is still God in the night

We talk of faith way up on the mountain
Talk comes so easy when life's at its best
Now down in the valleys, of trials and temptations
That's where your faith is really put to the test
For the God on the mountain is the God in the valley
When things go wrong, He'll make them right
And the God of the good times
Is still God in the bad times
The God of the day, is still God in the night
The God of the day, is still God in the night

Chapter Four

IF THERE'S HEALING IN THE ATONEMENT, WHY AM I STILL SICK?

As I struggled with my illness and all the implications and ramifications it held for my life, I immediately knew that there was one particular sermon that I needed to review.

During my ministry, I often heard Christians and even other pastors repeat the phrase, "There is healing in the atonement." It was used often in prayer meetings and in prayers for those who were sick as people claimed physical healing because of the promise, "by his stripes we are healed." Now I was on the receiving end of those prayers. But a couple years previously I had taken the time to dig more deeply into that issue, and as a result of that study, I had preached a sermon with the title: **If There Is Healing in the Atonement, Why Am I Still Sick?** Now I needed to listen to that sermon to see if it still held water and whether it provided the perspective and reassurance I had hoped to offer to others in times of physical illness.

I had chosen to preach on the subject on the week after Good Friday, when we, along with Christians around the world, had celebrated the truth of the atonement and the wonderful reality that "Christ died for our sins." But this was an additional claim growing out of the atonement, based on Isaiah 53:5 which reads, "and with his wounds (stripes) we are healed."

What follows is an edited version of what I shared with my congregation back in the spring of 2013.

The claim is sometimes made that there is healing in the atonement. That since there is healing in the atonement, since we are healed by his stripes and Jesus bore our diseases, then as followers of Christ, we should no longer experience physical disease. Such teaching sometimes goes on to tell us that physical disease is a work of the devil against us and an attack on our faith. We are therefore called on to exercise our faith and claim healing as a spiritual birthright as followers of Christ.

But will such teaching and such claims stand up to the light of day and to the light of Scripture? Very bluntly, my question is this: **If there is healing in the atonement, why are we still sick?**

Let's begin with the first part of that question. Is there healing in the atonement? The brief and simple answer to that question is: Or course there is! The Bible says so. "By his stripes we are healed." These words are not only found in Isaiah 53, but they are quoted in the New Testament in Matthew 8:17 and in 1 Peter 2:24.

But that answer does not take us very far. It does not address some very important, underlying questions. What kind of healing is in view, and when can we expect to experience it? So let me phrase the question a little differently. Based on the words of Isaiah 53, has God promised healing and good physical health to every believer who has the faith to claim it? One book that came out on this subject some years ago bore this title: **Jesus Wants You Well.** So I am asking, is that true? And if Jesus wants us well, why are so many of us still sick?

One common and obvious answer to that question, of course, is that we lack faith. "We have not because we ask not," as James tells us in James 4:2. Based on this answer, we are exhorted to ask and to ask in faith. But here is the problem. When healing doesn't come, our faith is then called into question. Herein lies the dilemma. This doctrine, which seems to offer so much hope to the suffering believer, becomes a two-edged sword for those experiencing chronic or life-threatening illnesses and disabilities. Because when healing doesn't come, the sufferer is left with the conclusion that it is his/her fault. They are sick because they lack faith. And so, to their physical suffering we add the emotions of guilt and failure.

So this is an important question that affects us all. Does God promise good health and healing to us as a spiritual birthright growing out of Christ's atoning death on the cross?

I asked the question earlier. Will this doctrine stand up to the light of day and the light of Scripture? I deliberately posed the question that way. I want to first look at it in the light of day. By that, I mean the light of real life and everyday experience of Christ's followers. I am painting broadly on a very large canvas, not focusing on individual stories or cases. I want to begin by taking the questions of physical health and illness, and relating them to the larger question of life and death.

Follow my reasoning as I pose a series of questions. Since the first century and the atoning death of Christ, how many of Christ's followers have died? I mean, physical death: their physical bodies stopped breathing and their soul left their bodies. How many? All of them, right? Except for those of us still living within our normal life spans today, every Christian in every generation for nearly 2000 years has died. The death rate for Christians is identical to the death rate for non-believers.

Now I ask this: what did these Christians die of? What was the cause of death? If there was a death certificate, what was written there? The causes vary. Some died in accidents or from injuries sustained in natural disasters. Some died in wars. Some died as martyrs, killed for their faithfulness to the name and cause of Christ. A happy few lived long lives, and died in their sleep in their own beds. But many, probably most, Christians died from some form of physical illness. They are the same illnesses that non-believers died of; things like Spanish flu, bubonic plague, diphtheria, tuberculosis, polio, cholera, malaria. It is an almost endless list. With the advance of modern medicine, many illnesses have been overcome in the developed world, but the death rate remains the same as people continue to die of things like heart disease, cancer, diabetes, and again the list goes on. We Christians are not immune. If there is healing in the atonement and "Jesus wants us well," why are we still dying of physical diseases? As we walk among the grave stones of these Christians, are we to conclude that they all died because of a lack of faith and believing prayer? What kind of comfort is that to offer the loved ones who weep beside those graves?

I do not think this doctrine stands up in the light of day and the realities of life and death that surround us. But of course, the real question for us is whether it will stand up in the light of Scripture. That is where I want to turn now. Let me explain my approach. I am not going to go to the particular Scriptures I quoted earlier in Isaiah 53 and the occasions when it is quoted in the New Testament. The reason I am not going to do that is that these verses alone will not answer our questions. I did a quick internet search on this question and found numerous articles and sermons on the subject on both sides of the issue, and they all went to these passages and made their points from them – only they reached different conclusions. It all boils down to a simple question of interpretation – whether you take the reference to healing as being physical healing of our bodies, or whether you take it to be spiritual healing from the dilemma of our sins. At the end of the day, the interpreter makes his call.

I want to step back from these Scriptures and consider the question of healing and physical health against the backdrop of a much broader issue. It is the issue of our expectations and spiritual birthright as members of the kingdom of God. As we consider this question, I believe it is vitally important that we understand the differences between what has been called the "now" and the "not yet" of the kingdom of heaven.

There are many Scriptures we can go to, but I want to focus primarily on two, both found in the writings of the Apostle Paul. The first is found in Romans 8:18-25. In the Biblical text below, I have inserted the distinctions between the "now" and the "not yet" of our inheritance.

[18] For I consider that the sufferings of this present time **(NOW)** are not worth comparing with the glory that is to be revealed to us **(NOT YET)**. [19] For the creation waits with eager longing **(NOW)** for the revealing of the sons of God **(NOT YET)**. [20] For the creation was subjected to futility **(NOW)**, not willingly, but because of him who subjected it, in hope [21] that the creation itself will be set free from its bondage to corruption and obtain the freedom of the glory of the

children of God **(NOT YET)**. [22] For we know that the whole creation has been groaning together in the pains of childbirth until now. **(NOW)** [23] And not only the creation, but we ourselves, who have the firstfruits of the Spirit **(NOW)**, groan inwardly **(NOW)** as we wait eagerly for adoption as sons, the redemption of our bodies. **(NOT YET)** [24] For in this hope we were saved. Now hope that is seen is not hope. For who hopes for what he sees? [25] But if we hope for what we do not see **(NOT YET)**, we wait for it with patience **(NOW)**.

We see throughout this passage an important distinction of our faith. There is a present reality and there is a future hope. The present reality (now) is described with such words as "suffering" and "groaning" and "pains of childbirth" while the future (not yet) is described with words like "glory" and "freedom". This glory and freedom is tied to something yet future that is described as "the redemption of our bodies." That tells us that our bodies are not yet fully redeemed or in their eternal state. These present bodies are still subject to suffering and decay and, yes, illness and disabilities. Yes, Christ's death has purchased our salvation. That salvation includes our physical bodies. But the full experience of that redemption is yet future. For now we have the firstfruits of the Spirit dwelling within us. But the fullness of our salvation is yet future and we are called on to "wait for it with patience."

The other passage I want to turn to is found in 2 Corinthians 4:7.

But we have this treasure in jars of clay, to show that the surpassing power belongs to God and not to us.

The treasure Paul is talking about is the new life in Christ – that we have the Spirit of God who is transforming us into the image of Christ. But for now, we hold this treasure in "jars of clay" which is a graphic image and metaphor for these present human bodies: fragile, often cracked and easily broken.
This thought continues if we skip down to verse 16:

So we do not lose heart. Though our outer self is wasting away, our inner self is being renewed day by day.

The "outer self" is a clear reference to our physical bodies. The distinction here is not between the now and the not yet, but between our physical bodies and our inner spirit. The one wastes away and grows increasingly weak, but our inner self can still thrive and be renewed. And the relative significance of these two realities is addressed in the next verse:

> 17 For this light momentary affliction is preparing for us an eternal weight of glory beyond all comparison, 18 as we look not to the things that are seen but to the things that are unseen. For the things that are seen are transient, but the things that are unseen are eternal.

So, living in the body, this "jar of clay" is described as "affliction" and "wasting away". There is no attempt to sugar coat that reality. But we are promised that this will be "light" and "momentary" compared to the eternal glory that awaits us.

That Paul is talking about the trials of living in our physical bodies is made clear in 2 Corinthians 5, beginning in verse 1:

> 1 For we know that if the tent that is our earthly home is destroyed, we have a building from God, a house not made with hands, eternal in the heavens. 2 For in this tent we groan, longing to put on our heavenly dwelling, 3 if indeed by putting it on we may not be found naked. 4 For while we are still in this tent, we groan, being burdened—not that we would be unclothed, but that we would be further clothed, so that what is mortal may be swallowed up by life. 5 He who has prepared us for this very thing is God, who has given us the Spirit as a guarantee.

Our physical body is described as a "tent". Tents are fragile and temporary. Once again there is a contrast between the "now" and the "not yet" of our inheritance. "Now" we live in a tent; we groan and we are burdened, longing for the "not yet" – that day when we shall put on our heavenly dwelling, a permanent building, a reference to our new body which we will receive when this life is over. We have the Spirit now as a guarantee, but the completeness of our inheritance is yet future.

The description of that future reality is truly glorious. Paul describes it in 1 Corinthians 15 as "this perishable body" putting on the "imperishable" and "this mortal body" putting on "immortality." Revelation 21:3-4 describes the believer's future this way:

> ³ And I heard a loud voice from the throne saying, "Behold, the dwelling place of God is with man. He will dwell with them, and they will be his people, and God himself will be with them as their God. ⁴ He will wipe away every tear from their eyes, and death shall be no more, neither shall there be mourning, nor crying, nor pain anymore, for the former things have passed away.

"No more mourning, crying or pain." That will be our new reality when the "former things have passed away." But that is future. That is "not yet." "Now" these realities are still with us, and physical illness and pain and death are part of that reality.

So how do we live now? How do we respond when illness comes and we experience the reality of physical pain and suffering in our bodies? How do we live "now" in light of the "not yet" of our inheritance. How do we respond to the words, "You have cancer!" Let me make 5 points.

1. We can accept the reality of the present age.

We should not be surprised, or react as though something strange or unexpected has come upon us. We live in a fallen world that is under the curse of sin, and we live in mortal bodies that are wasting away and will one day be torn down.

There is a great opening paragraph in a book that came out some years ago. The name of the book is **The Road Less Traveled** written by a psychologist named Scott Peck. I don't agree with all that is in the book, but I like the first paragraph:

Life is difficult. This is a great truth, one of the greatest truths. It is a great truth because once we truly see this truth, we transcend it. Once we truly know that life is difficult – once we truly understand and accept it – then life is no longer difficult. Because once it is accepted, the fact that life is difficult no longer matters.

One of the reasons life is difficult is that we live in these decaying "jars of clay." Accepting that as our present reality prepares us to face it and cope with it, rather than rail against it as something unexpected or unusual.

2. We can groan.

Did you ever see a child fall and skin his knee? If there are people around, he may be embarrassed and get up quickly, saying, "Didn't hurt!" But you can see from his trembling lip and welling tears that it really does hurt. Sometimes as Christians we feel that we have to deny the hurt or keep it inside, hidden away. We don't need to do that. Life hurts! Sometimes our bodies hurt. We should not be afraid to groan. After all, groaning is Biblical! That's what we saw in 2 Corinthians 5:4: "For while we are still in this tent, we groan, being burdened." We don't have to pretend it doesn't hurt. (By the way, there's a difference between groaning and whining!)

3. We can pray.

Sickness and pain should drive us to our knees. In 2 Corinthians 1, Paul talks about an experience he had in Asia when he despaired of life itself. We don't know if this was illness or not, but his response is important. He says in verse 9: "that was to make us rely not on ourselves but on God who raises the dead." And the way that we show our reliance on God is by praying. When you are sick, pray. When people you love are sick, pray. All the commands and instructions for prayer are applicable when we are sick. "Do not be anxious about anything, but in everything by prayer and supplication with thanksgiving let your requests be made known to God." Paul tells us in Philippians 4:5. And what is our request? I don't know about you, but when I am sick my request is that I will feel better; that I will be healed.

We can pray ourselves. We can also enlist others to pray. The Bible tells us to "pray for one another." And most wonderfully of all, we are promised the divine help of the Holy Spirit in our praying. In Romans 8, immediately following the passage we looked at a little while ago about "groaning along with the whole creation as we await the redemption of our bodies," we are offered this encouragement when we come to the end of our own praying. Let's read, starting in verse 26:

Likewise the Spirit helps us in our weakness.

By the way, in the original language, the word that is translated "weakness" is the very same word that is used in James 5:14, which is translated there as "Is anyone among you sick?" So we could translate this "Likewise the Spirit helps us in our sickness." Let's continue in Romans 8:

26 Likewise the Spirit helps us in our weakness. For we do not know what to pray for as we ought, but the Spirit himself intercedes for us with groanings too deep for words. 27 And he who searches hearts knows what is the mind of the Spirit, because the Spirit intercedes for the saints according to the will of God.

This is an important passage for us to consider. Not only are we promised the Holy Spirit's help in our praying, but we are also told that true and effective prayer is prayer "according to the will of God." That is why we need the Spirit's help. We don't always know what God's will is when we pray. But the Holy Spirit does. That introduces the understanding that healing may not always be God's will in every instance. That doesn't mean we stop praying. It means we pray differently. We pray, as Jesus did in the Garden of Gethsemane: "Not my will, but yours be done."

Praying "according to the will of God" is laid upon the strong foundation of the verse that follows:

> 28 And we know that for those who love God all things work together for good, for those who are called according to his purpose.

That leads me to the next point.

4. We can trust.

We pray urgently and fervently. We pray according to the will of God. And we trust God for the outcome. There are those who tell us that to pray "God's will be done" demonstrates a lack of faith. I would argue just the opposite. Praying for God's will to be done demonstrates great faith, because it does not just demonstrate faith in God's power to heal, but it demonstrates faith in his wisdom and his love and his sovereign plan should he choose not to heal. God's ways are not our ways and his thoughts are not our thoughts.

Finally,

5. We can live in hope.

For the followers of Jesus Christ, our response to illness and physical suffering is not that of fatalistic Stoicism and despair. It is built on the strong and certain belief in the "not yet" of our faith. Now we groan, but it is both a groan of pain and a groan of anticipation. We are waiting eagerly for our adoption ceremony, the redemption of our bodies. You see, our ultimate hope does not lie in physical healing. It lies in the return of Christ and the coming resurrection of our bodies.

It is the hope that Paul expresses in Philippians 3:20-21 when he says:

> But our citizenship is in heaven, and from it we await a Savior, the Lord Jesus Christ, who will transform our lowly body to be like his glorious body, by the power that enables him even to subject all things to himself.

It is "not yet" but it is coming. As Paul told us in Romans 8:24-25:

> For in this hope we were saved. For who hopes for what he sees? But if we hope for what we do not see, <u>we wait for it with patience.</u>

And so we are called to live in the "now", in mortal bodies, living by faith in God's power, his love and his wisdom, while relying on his sufficient grace and strength for each new day.

As I reviewed this sermon which I had preached over two years before, I reflected on it from my new reality. Now it was my turn. As I lay flat on my back, facing my own life-threatening illness and my own mortality, did I still believe what I had preached? Did I find the principles I had shared practical and encouraging? Was I standing on solid ground? The answer to these questions was a resounding "Yes."

But then I had some additional strong building blocks of faith to buttress my confidence. It was time to revisit an old friend.

Chapter Five
WHAT'S THE QUESTION?

Job is one of my favorite Bible characters, and an old friend. I have always been intrigued by his story. During my years as a pastor I have preached messages from the Book of Job on a number of different occasions. I will admit, though, when I would announce that I was planning a series on Job I would sometimes get a strange reaction. The person would get a rather panic-stricken look on his face. "Not a series of messages on Job," he might stutter. When I probed for the reason for the reaction, it often boiled down to a form of Christian superstition. The fear is that messages on Job are a harbinger of suffering that is about to come into their lives, almost as though the messages will somehow cause the suffering. The reality is that suffering comes into all of our lives in different forms and at different times. I hope you won't skip reading this chapter because of this fear. The difficult experiences of life will come whether you read it or not. It is my prayer that considering the message of Job's life will prepare you for those experiences by laying a strong foundation of Biblical faith.

In these chapters we have been considering the question of physical illness. I have been sharing my experience of walking through my own cancer diagnosis and subsequent illness and treatment. The question of illness, though, is just part of the larger question of pain and suffering of all kinds: grief and loss, tragedy and disaster. We have all known pain and suffering. We have suffered losses that we did not think we could endure. We have felt pain, both physical and emotional, that we did not think we could bear. In our pain and suffering we often wrestle with the question: "Why?"

It is a cosmic and global question. At its core it is a

profoundly theological question and a faith question. If God is good, if God is on his throne, if he is a loving God and if he is our God, why does he permit such suffering and pain to come into our lives? For me, this was now a very personal question. I had spent my life serving God. For forty years, I had served his church on three different continents. In serving, we had lived our lives separated from our parents and families, and later from our grown sons and our grandchildren. We had made sacrifices. Now, as we planned to wrap up our years of formal ministry and return to the US, I was facing cancer. It didn't seem fair.

In the Book of Job, the characters wrestle at length with these questions of pain and suffering and devastating losses. They wrestle particularly with a very specific question: Why do the righteous suffer? We can understand why "bad things happen to bad people." That kind of suffering makes sense. That's justice. They are getting what they deserve. But when bad things happen to good or seemingly innocent people, we struggle and want to know why. Particularly, when bad things happen to us, we want to know why. Job wrestled mightily with this question. So did his friends. So do we.

Before I go any further though, I must hasten to offer this disclaimer. As I began to review my messages from the Book of Job, I already knew that the book does not ultimately answer this question. The question is asked repeatedly in the book. There is much discussion of the matter. There are long discourses seeking to unravel the mystery. But when all is said and done, the question remains unanswered.

There is a reason for this. You see, the Book of Job was not written to answer the question, "Why do the righteous (God's followers) suffer?" In fact it was not written to answer a question at all but rather to ask a question. That question is this: **Why do the righteous worship?** Why do God's people worship and serve and obey him?

Let's set the stage. The Book of Job is part of the Wisdom Literature of the Old Testament, along with other books like Proverbs and Ecclesiastes. These books deal with some of the basic issues of life. Job is unique in the Scriptures as it is written in the form of a drama or play. It is based on real life events, but the telling is stylized to fit the dramatic setting with long speeches and dialogues. The drama takes place on two different sets or settings. One setting is on earth. The other is in heaven. We, as the viewers of the play, are privileged to see what goes on in both settings. It is as though we are watching events taking place on a stage, but there is a curtain running across the stage, perpendicular to those of us in the audience. We can see what is happening on the stage on both sides of the curtain. But it is vital to our understanding for us to realize that while we can see both settings and know what transpires in heaven as well as on earth, Job and his friends are never permitted that glimpse into the heavenly scene. In fact, even at the end of the story, Job still does not know about the discussion that took place in heaven. We must keep this in mind as the drama unfolds.

The story begins with a description of the main character in the drama:

> ¹ There was a man in the land of Uz whose name was Job, and that man was blameless and upright, one who feared God and turned away from evil. ² There were born to him seven sons and three daughters. ³ He possessed 7,000 sheep, 3,000 camels, 500 yoke of oxen, and 500 female donkeys, and very many servants, so that this man was the greatest of all the people of the east. ⁴ His sons used to go and hold a feast in the house of each one on his day, and they would send and invite their three sisters to eat and drink with them. ⁵ And when the days of the feast had run their course, Job would send and consecrate them, and he would rise early in the morning and offer burnt offerings according to the number of them all. For Job said, "It may be that my children have sinned, and cursed God in their hearts." Thus Job did continually (Job 1:1-5).

Job was not perfect. He will admit that in his own discourses later in the dialogue. But he was living an exemplary life of faith and obedience to God and a life of godly leadership in his own family. That is the scene on earth. But now the drama shifts to the scene in heaven.

> ⁶ Now there was a day when the sons of God came to present themselves before the Lord, and Satan also came among them. ⁷ The Lord said to Satan, "From where have you come?" Satan answered the Lord and said, "From going to and fro on the earth, and from walking up and down on it." ⁸ And the Lord said to Satan, "Have you considered my servant Job, that there is none like him on the earth, a blameless and upright man, who fears God and turns away from evil?" (Job 1:6-8)

Do you ever think of God bragging? It is not a term we often use in reference to God, but there is something that God takes pride in; something that gives him great satisfaction. That is the righteous lives of his people and the trust and confidence that they demonstrate in him. "Look at Job!" God says to Satan.

But now let's listen to Satan's cynical challenge in verses 9-11:

> ⁹ Then Satan answered the Lord and said, "Does Job fear God for no reason? ¹⁰ Have you not put a hedge around him and his house and all that he has, on every side? You have blessed the work of his hands, and his possessions have increased in the land. ¹¹ But stretch out your hand and touch all that he has, and he will curse you to your face."

This is the fundamental issue of the entire book. Why do the righteous worship? Why do they serve God? Why did Job fear God? Why was he living such a life of righteousness before God? Let's make it more personal. Why do I worship? Why do I serve God? Why do you worship and serve God?

There are two theses or answers to the question posed in this drama. God's answer is this: "My people (Job as a prime example) serve me because I am God. They worship me because I am worthy of worship. They obey out of love and reverence for me."

Satan snorts with cynical disgust. "No way! People only serve you because you pay good wages. People are essentially mercenaries. They only obey you because of the blessings you give. You can only win and keep human allegiance through bribery."

I am reminded of the phrase "rice Christians." It came from early missionary efforts. As missionaries preached the Gospel, out of genuine compassion they also offered food (rice) to feed the hungry. Over time they found the physical needs of the people exceeded their resources, so they began to limit their food distribution to those who joined the church. Suddenly lots of people were lining up to join the church! Only their faith was not sincere. They simply wanted to benefit from the rice distribution. Hence the phrase, "rice Christians." Essentially, Satan is accusing Job (and by implication, all who worship God) of being a "rice Christian." He is saying, "Take away your hand of blessing and protection and Job's faith and obedience will evaporate like the morning dew when the sun begins to shine."

So who is right? God or Satan? Whose prediction would stand up in Job's life? Whose prediction would stand up in your life or in mine?

So the stage is set and the trial is about to begin. Watch what happens next.

13 Now there was a day when his sons and daughters were eating and drinking wine in their oldest brother's house, 14 and there came a messenger to Job and said, "The oxen were plowing and the donkeys feeding beside them, 15 and the Sabeans fell upon them and took them and struck down the servants with the edge of the sword, and I alone have escaped to tell you." 16 While he was yet speaking, there came another and said, "The fire of God fell from heaven and burned up the sheep and the servants and consumed them, and

I alone have escaped to tell you." ¹⁷ While he was yet speaking, there came another and said, "The Chaldeans formed three groups and made a raid on the camels and took them and struck down the servants with the edge of the sword, and I alone have escaped to tell you." ¹⁸ While he was yet speaking, there came another and said, "Your sons and daughters were eating and drinking wine in their oldest brother›s house, ¹⁹ and behold, a great wind came across the wilderness and struck the four corners of the house, and it fell upon the young people, and they are dead, and I alone have escaped to tell you (Job 1:13-19).

The scope of the tragedy is almost beyond imagining. The scale of the disasters that fell upon Job defy our comprehension. We can picture the scene as it might play out on a stage. First one messenger arrives with his devastating news. Before he is even finished speaking, another messenger arrives, and then another and then another, until Job is utterly bereft of everything he held dear including, last of all, his sons and daughters.

Now the true drama of the play unfolds before us. How will Job respond? Who was right about Job? Was God right, or was Satan? Let's continue reading from Job 1:20-22.

²⁰ Then Job arose and tore his robe and shaved his head and fell on the ground and worshiped. ²¹ And he said, "Naked I came from my mother›s womb, and naked shall I return. The Lord gave, and the Lord has taken away; blessed be the name of the Lord." ²² In all this Job did not sin or charge God with wrong."

I get a lump in my throat when I read that. This is faith in action. God's own reputation and claims have been vindicated. If I may take some liberties, I suspect that God also had a lump in his throat and a tear in his eye when he saw Job's response. So the great test has been passed. But Satan is not through yet. The drama continues with another scene set in heaven:

¹ Again there was a day when the sons of God came

to present themselves before the Lord, and Satan also came among them to present himself before the Lord. ² And the Lord said to Satan, "From where have you come?" Satan answered the Lord and said, "From going to and fro on the earth, and from walking up and down on it." ³ And the Lord said to Satan, "Have you considered my servant Job, that there is none like him on the earth, a blameless and upright man, who fears God and turns away from evil? He still holds fast his integrity, although you incited me against him to destroy him without reason" (Job 2:1-3).

As God expresses his joy and pleasure in Job once again, Satan now makes an even more awful accusation.

⁴ Then Satan answered the Lord and said, "Skin for skin! All that a man has he will give for his life. ⁵ But stretch out your hand and touch his bone and his flesh, and he will curse you to your face" (Job 2:4-5).

Here is what Satan is actually saying: "Job is even worse than I thought. He doesn't even care about his family or anyone else. All he cares about is his own skin, his own physical health. But if you take that away, he will curse you."

⁶ And the Lord said to Satan, "Behold, he is in your hand; only spare his life." ⁷ So Satan went out from the presence of the Lord and struck Job with loathsome sores from the sole of his foot to the crown of his head. ⁸ And he took a piece of broken pottery with which to scrape himself while he sat in the ashes (Job 2:6-8).

This is the scene on earth. Totally unaware of the scene in heaven or what was at stake, Job now sat outside the city, in the city garbage dump. Everything is gone. He is now in great physical agony, scraping his boil-like sores with a broken shard of pottery. Then to top it all off, his own wife turns against him.

Then his wife said to him, "Do you still hold fast your integrity? Curse God and die" (Job 2:9).

It is difficult to imagine a scene of greater human misery. Once again, we hold our breath to see Job's response.

But he said to her, "You speak as one of the foolish women would speak. Shall we receive good from God, and shall we not receive evil?" In all this Job did not sin with his lips (Job 2:10).

To paraphrase Job's words, he says, "I will accept whatever God brings into my life, both the good and the bad, both the joy and the pain. I will trust in him because he is my God and he is worthy of my trust." And so Job demonstrated that God is able to evoke love, obedience and trust in his people apart from material considerations and physical blessings.

Job is one of my heroes. He wasn't a military hero. He wasn't a political leader. He never even pastored a great church or led a great Christian organization. But he won one of the greatest victories ever recorded for the kingdom of God. And he did not win that victory in front of a cheering multitude. He won that victory while seated on an ash heap outside the city with tears streaming down his face. What is more, when he won that victory, he didn't even know it. I suspect a cheer may have gone up in heaven, but Job didn't hear it. No trumpets sounded in his ears. No bells rang. He sat alone in great pain. Yet by his faith response, God's reputation and claims had been vindicated in the spiritual world.

But the drama of Job's life was not yet complete. In fact, in many ways, the real faith work was only beginning.

Chapter Six
GOOD THEOLOGY, BAD THEOLOGY

Every human being is a theologian. Everyone has a belief system which includes what we believe (or don't believe) about God; about the seen and unseen (spiritual) world and how they interact with each other. Each of us is faced constantly with the task of making sense of the world and our experiences in the world in light of our theology.

Even the atheist has a theology. He has studied the world around him and analyzed his own experiences and come to the conclusion that God does not exist. The person who believes in God must decide what kind of God he believes in and how this God works, and then seek to explain what happens around him in the light of his faith. That was the task that now faced Job and his friends; how to make sense of what has happened to Job in light of what they believed about God.

This was also the task that faced me as I lay in my hospital bed in Al Ain, United Arab Emirates. What did I believe about God? How could I reconcile what I believed with my present circumstances? Did my faith (belief) match my new reality of helplessness and intense pain?

The efforts of Job and his friends are recorded for us in Job 3-37. In this chapter we will only touch briefly on the highlights of the section in a kind-of satellite-view survey, but I encourage you to take the time to read the entire passage.

Job 3-37 is a section of Scripture that is filled with emotion. It is also filled with theology. Good theology and bad theology, as Job and his friends try to make sense of Job's tragedy, and to reconcile what has happened to Job with their theology and what they believe to be true about God. They are trying to match what they see with what they believe.

Let's set the stage from the end of Job chapter 2:

¹¹ Now when Job's three friends heard of all this evil that had come upon him, they came each from his own place, Eliphaz the Temanite, Bildad the Shuhite, and Zophar the Naamathite. They made an appointment together to come to show him sympathy and comfort him. ¹² And when they saw him from a distance, they did not recognize him. And they raised their voices and wept, and they tore their robes and sprinkled dust on their heads toward heaven. ¹³ And they sat with him on the ground seven days and seven nights, and no one spoke a word to him, for they saw that his suffering was very great.

We must remember from the story what they know and what they do not know. They were not privileged to see the scenes that took place in heaven; what happened on the other side of the curtain. They only saw the richest and greatest man they know seated on an ash heap; his wealth, his family and his health are all gone. It was as catastrophic a series of tragedies as any man has ever experienced. And their first response to Job and his grief is a good one. They simply sat silently and suffered with him.

But then in chapter 3 the great debate begins. Job speaks, and then his friends take turns in answering him. As you read this section, it is always very important to keep track of who is speaking. It is very easy to miss the forest for the trees in these chapters, and to lose the flow of what is being said by whom in the mass of verbal arguments.

Job opens with the first speech as chapter 3 begins:

¹ After this Job opened his mouth and cursed the day of his birth. ² And Job said:
³ "Let the day perish on which I was born,
and the night that said,
'A man is conceived.'
⁴ Let that day be darkness!
May God above not seek it,
nor light shine upon it."

And so Job continues throughout this chapter and many of his speeches that follow. He expresses the wish that he had never been born. Failing that, he wishes he had died at birth. Then he longs for death to take him now. "Why don't you let me die now, God?" he asks.

In these chapters we hear Job longing for the good old days, the days of his prosperity. "If only I could turn the clock back!" he implores. In his speeches, Job expresses disappointment and even anger at God. He cries out over and over to God for an explanation of what has happened.

The first thing that strikes me in these chapters is just how human Job was. I find that immensely reassuring. After reading the first two chapters, it would be possible to come away with the impression that Job was a figure carved from marble; a superhuman saint reacting to his great tragedies with great faith, almost as though unfazed by it all. But in the chapters that follow, when he opens his mouth and speaks, we find out how human he was; how like you and me he was in his reactions and feelings. I am reminded of the words of James in James 5 when he describes Elijah as "a man just like us." Or as the KJV translates, he was a "man of like passions."

Job was like us, a man of deeply felt emotions and questions and, yes, even doubts. Yet in spite of his human frailties and the turmoil of his emotions, Job's faith ultimately stood the test. As I read Job's words of protest again, I found them hugely encouraging. To be a man or woman of faith does not mean being a person without feelings, a woman without tears, a man without anger, a person without occasional times of experiencing a deep sense of disappointment in God. It is encouraging to discover that faith and human emotions are not mutually exclusive.

After Job's friends have sat silently with him for seven days, they listen to Job speak, and then they begin to offer their counsel and advice. When we left Job at the end of chapter 2, it seemed as though everything that could be taken away from him had been taken away: possessions, family, health and finally even the loving support of his own wife. What more could he lose? We are about to find out as we read this middle section of the Book of Job. There was one more thing that could be taken away and that is his reputation and respect in the community. Amazingly, it is this last shred of dignity that his friends now begin to attack.

Remember, Job's friends are doing what we all do. They are trying to make sense of the visible stuff of life in light of their theology or belief system. The theology of Job's friends can be summarized rather simply. God is a righteous and fair God. As a fair God, he rewards the righteous and punishes the wicked. Now they looked at Job, sitting like a beggar among the ashes, and they could only draw one conclusion. Job had sinned and God was punishing him. And because the punishment was great, therefore Job's sins must have been great. So in applying their logic and theology to the situation, they conclude that their role is to defend God's justice by exposing Job's sins and urging him to confess them. Only then would God restore his blessings.

Now, within their arguments there are many layers of logic and intricate reasoning, and even some subtle differences in the arguments of the different men, all of it stated in carefully crafted and beautiful Hebrew poetry. But it all essentially leads back to the same point: "Job, what have you done?"

Here is their basic presupposition:

⁷ Remember: who that was innocent ever perished?
Or where were the upright cut off?
⁸ As I have seen, those who plow iniquity
and sow trouble reap the same.
⁹ By the breath of God they perish,
and by the blast of his anger they are consumed
(Job 4:7-9).

Put very simply, God doesn't make mistakes. Therefore the fault must lie with Job.

The probing and the questioning goes on and on, chapter after chapter. In fact, as Job continues to protest his innocence, their attacks become more and more vicious. They begin to list all the sins they can think of and accuse Job of being guilty of them, without any evidence or basis in fact.

⁴ Is it for your fear of him that he reproves you
and enters into judgment with you?
⁵ Is not your evil abundant?
There is no end to your iniquities.
⁶ For you have exacted pledges of your brothers for nothing
and stripped the naked of their clothing.
⁷ You have given no water to the weary to drink,
and you have withheld bread from the hungry.
⁸ The man with power possessed the land,
and the favored man lived in it.
⁹ You have sent widows away empty,
and the arms of the fatherless were crushed.
¹⁰ Therefore snares are all around you,
and sudden terror overwhelms you,
¹¹ or darkness, so that you cannot see,
and a flood of water covers you (Job 22:4-11).

Understand! These things are not true! If they had been, God would never have described Job as a blameless and upright man who shunned evil. Job's friend is making them up, figuring Job has to be guilty of something, and if he just fires enough arrows, he is bound to hit on Job's hidden sins.

So how does Job respond to all of this? He cries out in wounded innocence. There are few things more painful than to suffer for something you have not done. But then to have people assume you did something wrong because you are suffering is to add the final measure of pain and indignity. The pain is now doubled!

In his response, Job is not claiming for himself total sinlessness. But what he does claim is that he is innocent of the terrible sins which would justify the awful things that have happened to him. He cries out over and over: "Lord, if I have sinned, show it to me and I will repent." But he refuses to confess what he has not done.

Job's defense reaches its climax in chapter 31:

⁵ If I have walked with falsehood
and my foot has hastened to deceit;
⁹ If my heart has been enticed toward a woman,
and I have lain in wait at my neighbor's door,
¹³ If I have rejected the cause of my manservant or my
maidservant,
when they brought a complaint against me,
¹⁷ If I have withheld anything that the poor desired,
or have caused the eyes of the widow to fail,
¹⁸ or have eaten my morsel alone,
and the fatherless has not eaten of it
²⁴ If I have made gold my trust
or called fine gold my confidence,
²⁵ if I have rejoiced because my wealth was abundant
or because my hand had found much,
²⁶ if I have looked at the sun when it shone,
or the moon moving in splendor,
²⁷ and my heart has been secretly enticed,
and my mouth has kissed my hand,
²⁸ this also would be an iniquity to be punished by the
judges,
for I would have been false to God above.
³³ if I have concealed my transgressions as others do
by hiding my iniquity in my heart,
³⁴ because I stood in great fear of the multitude,
and the contempt of families terrified me,
so that I kept silence, and did not go out of doors—
³⁵ Oh, that I had one to hear me!
(Here is my signature! Let the Almighty answer me!)
Oh, that I had the indictment written by my adversary!
³⁶ Surely I would carry it on my shoulder;
I would bind it on me as a crown;
³⁷ I would give him an account of all my steps;
like a prince I would approach him.

³⁸ "If my land has cried out against me
and its furrows have wept together,

³⁹ if I have eaten its yield without payment
and made its owners breathe their last,
⁴⁰ let thorns grow instead of wheat,
and foul weeds instead of barley."

In all of these verses, Job is saying one thing: "I will bear, even welcome, just punishment from the hand of God, but I cannot confess falsely to sins I have not committed."

And so the cycles of the debate continue, round and round, over and over.

Who is right and who is wrong?

The text of Job does come to our rescue on this question. I am going to cheat and skip to the answer at the back of the book. At the end of the day there is a divine answer, and God, as the judge of all and the final referee of all theological arguments, declares a winner in Job 42:7:

> After the Lord had spoken these words to Job, the Lord said to Eliphaz the Temanite: "My anger burns against you and against your two friends, for you have not spoken of me what is right, as my servant Job has."

So by God's own assessment, Job is right and his friends are wrong. But we are not told in just what way Job's friends erred. That is a question we must wrestle with and answer for ourselves. I was thankful, in my weakened state in the hospital, that I was not facing these questions for the first time. As he has so often in my life, God had prepared me ahead of time, through my own Bible study and sermon preparation. As I reviewed my sermon notes on the Book of Job, I found the following thoughts on why Job's friends erred.

1. Their understanding of God was incomplete.

They made a very common mistake. They assumed that God was as limited as their own concept of him; that what they understood about God was all there was to God. A man by the name of J. B. Philips wrote a book many years ago with the title: "Your God Is Too Small." In this book he talks about some of the misconceptions people have about God. One of those misconceptions he calls "God in a box." It is the idea that we take certain facts about God and from that we form our concept of God. Our concept of God becomes our box that we try to fit God into. Anything outside of the box gets cut off or ignored. No ambiguity is tolerated. This is what God is. This is how he acts. Our idea of God becomes our God.

Job's friends had put God in a box. It wasn't a bad box, as boxes go. They viewed God as a fair and righteous judge. But they also viewed him as a God who always works in very certain, predictable ways; ways that they could understand, manage and therefore control. But God is always bigger than our concept of him. God is always full of surprises. He is faithful to himself and to his character, but that does not mean that he is predictable by our measures of predictability. God's thoughts are not our thoughts and his ways are not our ways.

2. Their understanding of the world was incomplete.

They did not have a comprehensive enough view of the spiritual world and the forces at work on the "other side of the curtain." Satan was a vital player in this drama. Yet they had no idea what his role was or the effect that he had on Job's circumstances.

Now at this point it is hard to fault them. How could they know these things? We all have inadequate views of God, and what access did they have to the realities of the spiritual world? But their real error lay in a third point.

3. They made evaluations and passed judgments that they had neither qualifications nor sufficient facts to make.

Their chief problem lay in their assumption that they knew enough to explain God and condemn Job. In fact they were missing key pieces to the puzzle. They were missing an accurate knowledge of Job's personal life. So they made up things to fill in the gaps. They were missing the knowledge of Satan's role in the whole drama. They didn't know what God's ultimate plan and purpose was. They didn't know, and they didn't know what they didn't know. But they went ahead and made judgments anyway.

There is an important lesson for all of us to learn here. Don't pass judgment on others! We don't have enough facts. We never will have enough facts; either about their personal lives, about their struggles, about God's plan or purposes in their lives. Leave such judgments to God.

4. They failed to view the situation from the long-term, eternal viewpoint.

In order to understand God's justice and even attempt to balance it with our sense of fairness, we must keep the longest of long-term views. God's books will only close and be balanced in eternity. I have always liked the story of the two farmers who farmed adjacent fields. One was a committed Christian. The other was a godless man who lived only for his own pleasure. One year, as they gathered in their harvest it became obvious that the godless man had reaped a much more abundant crop. The Christian farmer had struggled with various disasters throughout the year, but the other man had been spared them all. When the harvest was complete the other man came to gloat. "Tell me. What good did all your praying and going to church do? Where is your God now? I don't even believe in God, let alone obey him. Yet I have double the harvest you have. How do you explain that?"

The Christian farmer answered simply: "God doesn't settle all of his accounts in October."

Well, what about Job? God said, "Job has spoken of me what is right." What did Job do right? Once again, I reflected on observations I had previously made from Job's example.

1. He was honest with God.

Here is where I could find myself connecting with Job in his humanness. I am not an overtly emotional person. Maybe it's my Scandinavian roots. But I did shed more than a few tears during those days. Some were simply physical tears in response to physical pain. But there were also emotional tears as Esther Ruth and I experienced loss after loss: long-anticipated trips canceled, plans changed, an altered sense of our future. I am a poor golfer, but I enjoy the game and was looking forward to playing more in retirement. Now the strength of my lower back was suspect and it was doubtful if I would be able to play again. I decided to give my clubs away. Somehow that act and the loss it signified slipped by my defenses and I broke down in tears. During the lonely nights in the hospital, I found myself complaining to God, just like Job.

It is important to remember that God can handle our honesty. Job is very transparent with his feelings; even his anger and his feelings of disappointment with God; his confusion and his tears. Yet God affirms him in the end. We don't have to hide our true feelings from God. He knows them anyway. Pour them out before God. He can handle them.

2. He clung to his faith in God in the midst of his pain.

We saw this in the previous chapter in Job's initial response to his tragedy. He continued in that faith through it all, even when that faith was stretched to the breaking point. In the midst of his pain, he utters these ringing words in Job 13:15: "Though he slay me, I will hope in him."

I believe he was able to do this, at least in part, because of this final point:

3. He trusted ultimately in his eternal hope.

There is another great statement of faith buried in all his confusion found in Job 19:23-27:

> [23] Oh that my words were written!
> Oh that they were inscribed in a book!
> [24] Oh that with an iron pen and lead
> they were engraved in the rock forever!
> [25] For I know that my Redeemer lives,
> and at the last he will stand upon the earth.
> [26] And after my skin has been thus destroyed,
> yet in my flesh I shall see God,

[27] whom I shall see for myself,
and my eyes shall behold, and not another.

Job is taking the longest of long-term views here. He is looking at life through the lens of eternity and holding on to his eternal hope; the hope of resurrection. Where did Job get this hope? What was his understanding of this word "Redeemer"? Did he know that he was prophesying about Jesus? I don't know the answer to these questions. I only know that buried in these tormented words of a suffering servant of God, we have these ringing words of faith as he clung to the eternal hope that has sustained true believers down through the centuries.

And now it was my turn. In the midst of my pain, and even my complaining, would my faith stand the test? I had advantages that Job didn't have. I know my Redeemer's name. His name is Jesus. I have multiple promises in the New Testament that clearly declare that for those who have trusted in Jesus as Savior, "to be absent from the body is to be present with the Lord." But it still took an active step of faith to take my eyes off the immediate circumstances and fix my sight on the eternal promises of God. It was a step I had to take repeatedly when the pain came in waves and the losses (or prospective losses) continued to mount.

Chapter Six

WHEN GOD ASKS THE QUESTIONS

N ow it was time for me to review the conclusion to the Book of Job. Would I find the answers I was looking for? Would the answers satisfy me in my new, "cancer" circumstances?

Life is filled with "Why?" questions. You only have to listen to the news reports. Hurricanes, floods, fires, droughts. Then there are the man-made disasters: mass shootings, senseless wars, domestic abuse, the list goes on and on.

And we ask, "Why?"

As a Christian who believes the Bible, I knew I had at least a partial, big picture answer to these questions. We know, from Genesis 3 and the account of the fall of Adam and Eve and the chapters that follow, that we live in a broken, fallen world that has been subjected to futility and frustration; it is a world under a curse because of mankind's rebellion against God, the Creator. What we see in the larger world around us are the consequences of sin and the fall of man, resulting in our alienation from God.

While that answer may partially satisfy us at the cosmic, macro level, if you're like me, we can still struggle with the "Why?" question on the individual, micro level. Why these people? Why that country? Why children? Why this? And, particularly pressing and personal, "Why me? Why cancer? Why now?"

I remember many years ago, sitting and listening to the prayer of a man who was in the midst of an excruciating personal tragedy. I still remember his prayer that day. "Lord, we can accept anything from your hand, but we have to know why."

In this final chapter dealing with the Book of Job, we find

that Job was also troubled by that question. In the chapters we have considered, Job marvelously affirmed his faith in God, but he shouts repeatedly to heaven, just as that man did in his prayer: "Why, God? Why? I have to know why!"

Here is a sample of Job's protesting cry as recorded in Job 23:1-5:

¹ Then Job answered and said:

² "Today also my complaint is bitter;
my hand is heavy on account of my groaning.
³ Oh, that I knew where I might find him,
that I might come even to his seat!
⁴ I would lay my case before him
and fill my mouth with arguments.
⁵ I would know what he would answer me
and understand what he would say to me.

Job demands an audience with God, so that he can make his case and argue with God and demand an answer from God.

And so, following chapter after chapter of agonizing debate, the Book of Job reaches its climactic moment. In the final chapters, God shows up. We are told in Job 38:1 that he showed up in a unique way. It says that the Lord answered Job out of the whirlwind. NIV translates it "storm". The basic meaning is a strong wind. My own picture of it is a kind of mini twister or tornado funnel – intense, but localized. We used to see these in Africa from time to time – just a sudden funnel of wind that would spring up and lift dust, leaves and other debris high into the air. This is the same word that is used to describe the wind (or whirlwind) that took Elijah up to heaven.

Whatever the mode of his appearance, it is what he said that makes the deepest impression.

² Who is this that darkens counsel by words without knowledge?
³ Dress for action like a man;
I will question you, and you make it known to me"
(Job 38:2-3).

In God's opening words, the whole perspective and orientation of the Book of Job and indeed of the universe itself is turned upside down and inside out. Job has been asking and demanding answers from God. When God shows up, he says simply: "Here I am, but I will be the one asking the questions and you will answer me."

I am reminded of a common scene in many police shows on TV. The suspect in a crime has been apprehended, and he starts asking; "Why am I here? Why are you arresting me? What evidence do you have against me?" And the arresting officer says quietly, "I will be the one asking the questions!"

Why do I say that these words turn the perspective of the Book of Job and even the universe inside out? We tend to view the universe and life and life's circumstances from a man-centered and self-centered perspective. We are the center of the universe. God exists to serve us and to meet our needs. And when he does not fulfill our expectations, we demand that he explain himself to us. This is what Job has been doing. But God refuses to answer any of Job's questions. In these chapters, there is not even one hint of an effort to explain to Job what was going on or what had happened in the scenes behind the curtain. God felt no obligation whatsoever to answer Job's questions. "I will ask the questions," he says. "You will answer me."

We will never understand the Book of Job until we realize that it is not a man-centered book. It is a God-centered book. Job is not the main character in the story. God is. God is the sun. Job is simply one of the planets. And I would go further and state that we will never understand the Bible until we realize that it is not a man-centered book, but a God-centered book. And we will never begin to understand life and the world around us until we realize that this world, this universe is not man-centered. It is God-centered. He created it. He rules it. He is sovereign. And as the Sovereign One, he will ask the questions.

So what does God do for Job, if he does not answer his questions? He takes him on a tour of nature and the created world. In these chapters, we have some of the most exquisite poetry in the Bible, as God's questions are put into beautiful images and figurative descriptions of the created world. We are just going to sample a few. In chapter 38, he begins by describing the beauty and power of inanimate nature.

> ⁴ Where were you when I laid the foundation of the
> earth?
> Tell me, if you have understanding.
> ⁵ Who determined its measurements—surely you
> know!
> Or who stretched the line upon it?
> ⁶ On what were its bases sunk,
> or who laid its cornerstone,
> ⁷ when the morning stars sang together
> and all the sons of God shouted for joy?
> ⁸ "Or who shut in the sea with doors
> when it burst out from the womb,
> ⁹ when I made clouds its garment
> and thick darkness its swaddling band,
> ¹⁰ and prescribed limits for it
> and set bars and doors,
> ¹¹ and said, 'Thus far shall you come, and no farther,
> and here shall your proud waves be stayed'?
> (Job 38:4-11)

He goes on to describe the wonders of climate and weather and the marvels of the animal world. This section of the Book of Job is one of my favorites, with verse after verse of beautiful poetry and descriptions that often recall scenes from my growing-up years in East Africa.

Throughout the section, God keeps asking Job the questions: Did you create this? Can you do this? Can you make this happen? Do you understand how this works?

He then returns to his challenge in chapter 40:1-2:

> ¹ And the Lord said to Job:
> ² "Shall a faultfinder contend with the Almighty?

He who argues with God, let him answer it."

"Job, do you really want to argue with me? Do you really want to debate me? Do you really want to question me and the way I run the universe?"
In awe, Job bows in worship:

³ Then Job answered the Lord and said:
⁴ "Behold, I am of small account; what shall I answer you?
I lay my hand on my mouth.
⁵ I have spoken once, and I will not answer;
twice, but I will proceed no further" (Job 40:3-5).

To be sure that the lesson has gone home, God challenges Job again:

⁶ Then the Lord answered Job out of the whirlwind
and said:
⁷ "Dress for action like a man;
I will question you, and you make it known to me.
⁸ Will you even put me in the wrong?
Will you condemn me that you may be in the right?
⁹ Have you an arm like God,
and can you thunder with a voice like his?
(Job 40:6-9)

He then goes on to ask Job: Do you want to govern the world? Do you think you can do a better job?

¹⁰ Adorn yourself with majesty and dignity;
clothe yourself with glory and splendor.
¹¹ Pour out the overflowings of your anger,
and look on everyone who is proud and abase him.
¹² Look on everyone who is proud and bring him low
and tread down the wicked where they stand.
¹³ Hide them all in the dust together;
bind their faces in the world below.
¹⁴ Then will I also acknowledge to you
that your own right hand can save you (Job 40:10-14).

God asks Job, "Do you think it is easy being God? Do you want to take my place? If you are wiser and more powerful than I am? I will be glad to give you a turn!"

It is vital for us to notice at this point that God has not answered a single one of Job's questions. He has not taken Job into his confidence about the scenes in heaven, or revealed the role that Satan has played in the trial – or even the honor that Job has brought to God's name by holding onto his faith in the midst of trial. In response to all of Job's protests and questions, God has really only said one thing to Job:

"I am God. Consider my greatness, my majesty, my power, my wisdom as displayed in the things that I have made. And worship me, simply because I am God."

We see Job's response in Job 42:1-6

¹ Then Job answered the Lord and said:
² "I know that you can do all things,
and that no purpose of yours can be thwarted.
³ 'Who is this that hides counsel without knowledge?'
Therefore I have uttered what I did not understand,
things too wonderful for me, which I did not know.
⁴ 'Hear, and I will speak;
I will question you, and you make it known to me.'
⁵ I had heard of you by the hearing of the ear,
but now my eye sees you;
⁶ therefore I despise myself,
and repent in dust and ashes."

And so, with his questions unanswered but his faith intact, Job bowed in humble worship before the God of the universe; the Creator God, his God, the God who can do all things and whose purposes cannot be thwarted.

We came to the Book of Job with the question: Why do the righteous suffer? But we very quickly discovered that that is not the question that the Book of Job was written to address. Instead it was written to raise a different question: Why do the righteous worship?

And as the chapters have unfolded, we discovered

something else. We thought we came to this book to ask God questions and demand answers. Instead, we found that the Book of Job was actually written to ask each of us a question. And that question is very personal and very profound: Whom do I worship? Whom do you worship? And why do we worship him?

As I reviewed the sermons I had preached on Job, I recognized that in my cancer, it was not I who was asking God questions. It was God who was questioning me. The pain I experienced during those weeks in the hospital was unlike anything I had felt before. I couldn't do anything for myself. The least physical movement would set off spasms of intense pain in both hips; pain that literally took my breath away.

In the midst of the pain, Job's words came back to me: "Shall we receive good from God, and shall we not receive evil?" Why did I worship God? Whose thesis was right: God's or Satan's? Was I a "rice Christian" offering my trust and reverence to God only on the good days, when the sun shone brightly? I had enjoyed a lifetime of good health. I had gladly accepted this good gift from God. Was I now willing to love and trust him when that good gift was taken away and replaced with this searing pain? Was I willing to trust him, even when it didn't make sense? Was I ready to trust him, even when it didn't seem fair? Was I able to trust him, even if I didn't know why? These were no longer hypothetical questions. They were questions that demanded an answer.

There was a Christian film that came out many years ago called The Hiding Place. It tells the true story of Corrie ten Boom. She belonged to a family of believers in Holland during the 2nd World War. This family risked their lives by hiding Jews from the Nazis. Ultimately, they were discovered and arrested and sent to a concentration camp where the father and one of the two sisters, named Betsy, were eventually put to death. The other sister, Corrie, survived to tell their story and to have a world-wide ministry of writing and speaking.

There is one particular scene in the film that powerfully imprinted itself on my memory. It takes place in the concentration camp. Corrie and Betsy have become known as Christians, which has subjected them to considerable scorn from the other, embittered residents of the camp. How could anyone cling to faith in God under such horrendous conditions? One of the women was especially bitter.

"I am a violinist," she said. "I spent years in lessons and practice. I became one of the best. I played first violin in one of the finest orchestras in Europe. And now look!"

She thrust her hands out in front of her. They were gnarled and crooked. Practically every bone in her hands had been broken under Nazi torture. "I will never play the violin again," she said. "If there is a God, why did he permit this to happen? Why? Why?"

There was a long silence. Then Betsy answered, very softly and very simply: **"If you know him, you don't have to know why."**

That's really the whole practical application of the Book of Job in a single sentence. If we know God, we don't have to know why. Job demanded answers. "Tell me why, God! Tell me why!" When God appeared, he said to him simply: "Look at me Job. Consider what I have made. Meditate on me and on my wisdom and my power." And when Job looked at God, he no longer needed to know why. It was enough just to know God.

And so the story concludes. With Job's faith intact and affirmed and God's question (not Job's) answered, God set out to restore Job. He opened the windows of heaven and began to pour out blessings once again. All his possessions were restored twice over, and in the process of time, ten more children were born to him.

We need this encouragement during the times of testing and despair. When the time of our testing is past, God will restore us and lift us up. He will often do it in this life, and he will certainly do it in the life to come.

Not everyone is satisfied with the answers the Book of Job gives. I remember taking a literature class in university, in which we studied Job as a piece of literature. It was interesting to listen and participate in a discussion on the Book of Job with people who were not believers. I remember one outspoken student. His summary of the Book of Job was laced with profanity and obscenities: "I think Job was #*&#, &#*#, *!#*# stupid!"

He spoke as one who did not know God. To unconditionally trust a God whom we do not know is impossible.

Yes, I have had a lifetime of following the Lord. It has been a lifetime of obedience and trust. Without trying to sound arrogant, I can say that in that lifetime, I have come to know God. And so I could say, "Yes, Lord, I trust you, even in my pain, even with my cancer."

Maybe you are still where my classmate in college was. You don't know God. He is a stranger to you, and an object of fear, or bitterness, or confusion or all three. It's no wonder you can't trust him. But how can you get to know him? Where can you go to find him?

God appeared to Job and took him on a tour of the created world to reveal his power and wisdom and to inspire Job's trust. That is one very good way to know God and to reflect on his greatness. Walk out at night and look up at the stars. Examine the intricate petals of a tiny flower. Listen to the thunder and watch the lightning flash and consider the works of God.

But there is an even better way. In John 14:8, one of Jesus' disciples named Philip approached Jesus with a request.

> [8] Philip said to him, "Lord, show us the Father, and it is enough for us."

That sounds like a reasonable request. Maybe he had one of the Old Testament accounts of God's appearances in mind. Maybe he was even thinking of God's appearance to Job in the whirlwind. "Show us the Father, and it is enough."

How did Jesus respond?
> [9] Jesus said to him, "Have I been with you so long, and you still do not know me, Philip? Whoever has seen me has seen the Father."

Paul says it this way in Colossians 1:15a: "He is the image of the invisible God."

He adds in Colossians 1:19: "For in him (Jesus) all the fullness of God was pleased to dwell."

If you want to know God, you need to get to know Jesus. My walk of faith began when I was just a child. It was faith in Jesus as my personal Savior. Jesus is the Word become flesh; God the invisible in visible form. He is the Way to the Father. Open a Bible and start to read. Start with one of the Gospels. Before you read, pray this simple prayer: "God, I want to know you. Show yourself to me." If you will do this with an open heart and mind, be ready for the adventure of a lifetime.

Be careful, though. You may think you are coming to ask God questions. But don't be too surprised if you soon find that it is God who is asking you the questions!

Chapter Eight

WHEN GOD SAYS NO

The subject of prayer has come up several times in earlier chapters. One of the applications I made for responding to illness (as to any other difficult challenge in life) is to pray and "make our requests known to God." This was indeed my first response to my cancer diagnosis. I am grateful to say that I was not alone in this response. The whole congregation joined with me in praying. On the evening that had been planned for our all-church farewell, I was flat on my back in the hospital, unable to move. Instead of canceling the event, the congregation gathered together to pray for me. We were all praying for a miracle and for quick and total healing.

In the days and weeks that followed, those prayers continued. An international church is not only international, it is also transient. We had former church members scattered around the world. As news of my illness spread through the network, we received messages of comfort and support from every continent (except Antarctica – someone needs to get down there and teach those penguins to pray!). All of those messages included the fact that people were praying for me – and they were praying for a miracle.

So, did God answer our prayers? The answer to that question is both yes and no. What do I mean by that, and how do I make sense of it? That was the matter I now faced. Once again I turned back to a previous sermon I had preached; one of a series of sermons on the topic of prayer.

One of the most helpful things I ever learned about prayer was something I was taught when I was still quite young. It was the fact that God always answers our prayers. But he may answer them in one of three ways: Yes, No and Wait. It is a simple lesson – one that I could grasp even as a child. But it still remains a very helpful truth to keep in mind as we consider God's response to our petitions and requests.

Back to my cancer, and my own prayers and those on my behalf. We saw many answers to prayer during those painful and dark days. God was very present, and his providence and his provision for my needs through doctors and others was wonderful to see and experience. But did I see a miracle, an instantaneous and dramatic removal of my cancer? No, I did not.

In wrestling with this fact, the passage of Scripture that helped me the most is found in 2 Corinthians 12:1-10. In this passage, Paul describes a powerful spiritual experience he had had 14 years previously. It was the kind of experience that the Corinthian believers took great delight and pride in. It was an up-close-and-personal encounter with the power of God. Such experiences may sometimes have the undesirable effect of producing a sense of pride and spiritual superiority. But in this case, as Paul narrates, to keep that from happening he was given what he refers to as a "thorn in the flesh."

This passage has always intrigued interpreters. What was Paul's thorn? Various possibilities have been suggested. They include various physical maladies such as epilepsy, periodic bouts of depression, migraine headaches, severe eye trouble, malaria, or possibly a stutter or some kind of speech impediment. Others have suggested some chronic, strong compulsion or temptation or even a personality disorder that he could never fully conquer.

The bottom line is that we don't know what Paul's thorn in the flesh was. I believe God intended it this way. If we knew what Paul's thorn was, we would have a tendency to draw comparisons. "Well, that is not so bad compared to what I have to put up with," we might be tempted to say. By not knowing what it is, Paul's thorn becomes a symbol for all the chronic troubles of the human experience.

So, what did Paul do about it? He did exactly what all of us should do. He prayed. Verse 8 says:

Three times I pleaded with the Lord about this, that it should leave me.

When Paul says that he did this three times, I don't think he means that he mentioned it as a prayer request on three different occasions. I think it means that three times he engaged in extended sessions of prayer and probably fasting. He engaged in serious supplication. He says he "pleaded" with the Lord. This is a strong word, full of urgency and strong emotion – to plead, beg, entreat – use any synonym you want.

So, how did God answer? Let's look at the next verse.

⁹ But he said to me, "**NO!** My grace is sufficient for you, for my power is made perfect in weakness."

Now, I will admit, if you compare this with what is written in your Bible, the word "NO" is not in the text. It is not found in the original manuscripts either. But it is there nonetheless by implication. Paul asked that the thorn in the flesh would leave, and it did not leave. Bottom line: God said NO!

We don't like the word "NO" do we? We want what we want and we want it now. When God says "No" or even when he just says, "Wait" we tend to get upset and to throw ourselves a pity party.

I believe it is at such times that we need to ask God to give us a teachable spirit to learn the lessons that he is trying to teach us. God is never arbitrary or capricious in his dealing with us. He is always purposeful. It is just that his purposes are sometimes different than ours.

From Paul's example here as well as his other writings, I would like to suggest four potential lessons we can learn when God says "No."

The first lesson is a paradoxical one.

Lesson # 1: We are strong when we are weak.

Or, as Paul puts, "God's strength is made perfect in weakness." This was the answer that God gave to Paul. "My power is made perfect in weakness."

This takes us back into the story of Paul and his vision. As he ruminated on the thorn in his flesh, he came to understand its purpose.

> So to keep me from becoming conceited because of the surpassing greatness of the revelations, a thorn was given me in the flesh, a messenger of Satan to harass me, <u>to keep me from becoming conceited</u>. (verse 7)

He goes on in a similar vein in the following verses:

> ⁹ Therefore I will boast all the more gladly of my weaknesses, <u>so that the power of Christ may rest upon me.</u> ¹⁰ For the sake of Christ, then, I am content with weaknesses, insults, hardships, persecutions, and calamities. For <u>when I am weak, then I am strong</u>.

How does this paradox work? It is a difficult one to wrap our minds around. Simply put, when we feel strong, we tend to rely on our own strength. So that is really all we have to offer – our own strength, and with it often comes pride in our achievements. It all becomes about us.

It is when we are aware of our weakness that we rely upon the power of Christ. Then it is his magnificent power that shines through our weakness, and it all becomes about Christ and his glory.

Earlier, in chapter one, Paul reflects on another experience he had when he thought he was going to die. It's recorded in 2 Corinthians 1:8-9:

> ⁸ For we do not want you to be unaware, brothers, of the affliction we experienced in Asia. For we were so utterly burdened beyond our strength that we despaired of life itself. ⁹ Indeed, we felt that we had received the sentence of death...

From that experience he drew this lesson:

> But that was <u>to make us rely not on ourselves but on God </u>who raises the dead.

So that is one reason God may allow trials to come into our lives and why he may answer "No" to our petitions that they be removed. He wants to display his power through us – and he can do this best when we are fully aware of our own weakness.

The second lesson that God may be trying to teach us when he says "No" is…

Lesson # 2: The secret of contentment

For this related lesson, I want to turn to Philippians 4:11-13.

> [11] Not that I am speaking of being in need, for I have learned in whatever situation I am to be content. [12] I know how to be brought low, and I know how to abound. In any and every circumstance, I have learned the secret of facing plenty and hunger, abundance and need. [13] I can do all things through him who strengthens me.

How does this passage relate to our subject of "When God Says No"? Oftentimes, we go to the Lord with our requests and with our needs. We go to him to seek the things that we believe will make us content. But in this passage, Paul takes us deeper into the secret of contentment, and he tells us it is not about what we have or don't have. As he says: "I have learned in whatever situation I am to be content." He is not just talking about poverty and riches but about all of life's circumstances of prosperity or adversity. "In any and every circumstance I have learned the secret of facing plenty and hunger, abundance and need."

So here is the question before us. What is the secret Paul learned? It took me a long time to see it, but it's found right here in plain view in this passage. The secret is verse 13: "I can do all things through him who strengthens me."

One of the reasons it took me so long to discover this secret is because this is one of those verses that has become isolated from its context. Frankly, a lot of very foolish and absurd claims have been made by preachers using this verse as their authority.

The other reason we miss the connection is because of a difficulty in translation. Let me explain. The first thing we need to know is that the word "do" is not in the Greek text. What the original literally says is, "I can...all things..." But that makes no sense in English, does it? It is incomplete. So the translators have provided a helping verb to complete the meaning. As is often the case in such contexts, they have used a very neutral, non-specific verb, "do". But unfortunately, when we translate it that way and we isolate this verse from its context, we can find ourselves far off course.

I sympathize with the translators, because it is not easy to render this verse clearly into English. But I would suggest supplying some different verbs in light of the context of contentment, poverty and plenty, of good circumstances and difficult circumstances. How about, "I can (endure) all things..."? Or maybe, "I can (cope) with all things..."The best published translation I found was J.B. Phillips: "I am ready for anything..." But then I settled on the simplest solution, by simply relying on the words in the context itself. "I can (be content) in every circumstance..." He is simply repeating his premise and setting us up for the secret he is about to deliver. Here it is. Are you ready for it? "Through him (Christ) who strengthens me."

The secret is the indwelling Christ and the strength that he provides. He dwells in me. He is my constant companion in every situation and in every circumstance. With him beside me, I have all I need. I am content because I know that he will supply all the strength I need to endure, to persevere and to overcome whatever comes my way. This is the lesson we need to learn when God says "No" or "Wait" to our requests. We can rely on the strength of Christ living in us. If we have him, we have all we need.

We might ask, "Where and when did Paul learn this secret of being content in any and all circumstances?" I don't think it is too much of a stretch to suggest that he learned it on his knees when God said "No" to his request to remove his thorn in the flesh. The word for "strengthen" found in the Philippians passage comes from the same root as the word strength that Paul discovered in 2 Corinthians 12, when he learned that this "strength was made perfect in weakness." He received God's answer, and learned that lesson and because of it, he was content. It was a lesson and a secret that he could and did then apply to any and every circumstance.

This brings us naturally to the third lesson we can learn:

Lesson # 3. The sufficiency of God's grace.

This really brings the previous two points together. And this was the lesson Paul learned from the Lord in 2 Corinthians 12:9:

> But he said to me, "My grace is sufficient for you…"

There is a tight linguistic connection here that comes through in the original Greek language Paul used when he wrote. The word "sufficient" found here and the word "content" in the passage in Philippians both come from a common root. It is a word that means "enough" or if we could coin a phrase, "a state of enoughness." When we pray and we persevere in prayer, we may not get exactly what we are asking for – but we will receive God's grace and we will experience the strength which Christ supplies, and that will be enough, and more than enough.

Look at how Paul concludes his thoughts after receiving this answer from the Lord in 2 Corinthians 12:

> [9] Therefore I will boast all the more gladly of my weaknesses, so that the power of Christ may rest upon me. [10] For the sake of Christ, then, I am content with weaknesses, insults, hardships, persecutions, and calamities. For when I am weak, then I am strong.

He not only accepted God's answer. He embraced it and learned to rejoice in it – reveling, as it were, in his own weakness because it provided such an ideal platform for the power of Christ to be displayed.

That brings us to the fourth lesson we can learn when God says "No."

Lesson # 4: Trust in God

At the end of the day, this is the primary lesson of the Bible, from Genesis to Revelation. It is a question that is posed to us again and again throughout life's journey. Can God be trusted? It is a question that is presented to us with unique urgency and poignancy when we face one of God's "No" answers. Can God be trusted? Can we trust his power? Can we trust his wisdom? Can we trust his timing? Do we trust his love?

These are not theoretical questions. These are real life questions. And these are questions which probe the deepest corners of our hearts.

I am reminded of the passage we considered in an earlier chapter: Proverbs 3:5 states:

Trust in the Lord with all your heart,
and do not lean on your own understanding.

That is where the challenge lies, especially when God's says, "No" to our petitions. Will we trust in the Lord, or lean on our own understanding?

The Bible makes clear that these will often be at odds with one another. In a verse I have quoted before from Isaiah 55:8-9 we read:

8 For my thoughts are not your thoughts,
neither are your ways my ways, declares the Lord.
9 For as the heavens are higher than the earth,
so are my ways higher than your ways
and my thoughts than your thoughts.

So where does our trust lie? In our own thoughts or in God's thoughts? In our ways or God's ways? When God says "No" to our prayers, he is giving us an opportunity to learn in new ways to trust him. He is our Father in heaven. And our Father knows best.

I had my first opportunity to experience the truths

expressed in this chapter in the weeks immediately following my diagnosis. I was able to come out of hospital and preach one more time at the end of November. Because of my weakness and lingering pain, I needed help to come out on the platform. It hurt too much to sit, so I preached from a standing position, holding onto a walker. Yet in my visible, physical weakness, I sensed a great strength; Christ's strength. As I preached, I sensed the congregation leaning in (physically and spiritually) to listen. My physical weakness amplified my words of testimony. Many wrote to me afterwards to testify to the impact of that message. Christ's strength was made perfect in my weakness.

I have continued to reflect on these truths and the questions of answered and unanswered prayer. As I write this chapter, two years have passed. Has God answered my prayers (and the prayers of many others on my behalf)? My first answer is, "Yes!" He did not answer them by miracle, but rather by his providence.

I spent three extra months in UAE receiving the first rounds of chemotherapy. The tumor was reduced through radiation. The pain receded. I was able to get back on my feet. We then relocated to Oregon (our original retirement destination) where I entered the care of the Oncology department at the Oregon Health and Science University (OHSU) in Portland. There I underwent a stem cell transplant (often referred to as a bone marrow transplant). Time and this chapter are not enough to relate all the answers to prayer we experienced: places to stay, excellent doctors, insurance that covered expenses. Even more importantly, my body responded well to all the treatments. The chemo reduced the bad blood numbers and prepared me for the transplant. The side effects of the transplant were kept to a minimum. I experienced no complicating infections. I was released from the hospital after 12 days (a normal stay is 14 to 21 days). After 90 days the doctors declared that my cancer was officially "in remission." It took time, but my strength returned and I feel good. To all of these things, I say, "Praise the Lord!" and attribute them to answered prayers.

But there is another side to the story. The doctors tell me that "remission" and "cure" are not synonymous. With this particular cancer, one doctor told me, "It will come back." The only question is when. I also walk with a limp. The original tumor caused some damage to the sciatic nerve that has left one leg weak. The chemo has also caused lingering numbness in both feet. I have prayed about all of these things and asked God to take them away. I continue to seek the best help that the medical professionals can offer. But until now God has said "No" or "Wait" to these requests.

So I go back to 2 Corinthians 12 and find comfort. I embrace my weakness and ask that God's strength will be displayed through it. I review the secret of contentment in Philippians 4 and know that I can endure anything (and be content) because Christ is the one who strengthens me.

The lyrics of a contemporary Christian song by Laura Daigle have been running through my head recently. It's called "I Will Trust." My heart particularly resonates with the words of the chorus:

> *When you don't move the mountains*
> *I'm needing you to move*
> *When you don't part the waters*
> *I wish I could walk through*
> *When you don't give the answers as I cry out to you*
> *I will trust, I will trust, I will trust in you!*

Chapter Nine
THAT'S HEAVY!

As I sat in the oncologist's office and heard the word "cancer", the first thing I faced (along with every other person who receives a life-threatening diagnosis) was the fact of my own mortality. Everyone dies. We all know that. But we tend to think that it happens to old people, ill people, and most importantly, other people. But when I heard the word "cancer" and reviewed the prognosis of my disease, it was no longer something that just happened to other people. It was something that was going to happen to me, and very possibly sooner than I was expecting.

That idea takes some getting used to. As I faced that reality, I found my faith in Jesus Christ and his death and resurrection to be a great comfort. I believe the Bible to be true and John 3:16 took on new and very personal meaning:

> For God so loved the world, that he gave his only Son, that whoever believes in him should not perish but have eternal life.

In the first chapter, I wrote about the simplicity of life that comes when we know the answer to two basic questions: What is life for? What comes after? Philippians 1:21 says it clearly where Paul writes:

> For to me to live is Christ, and to die is gain.

Based on the promises of the Bible, I found that I had no fear of death because I knew that what would come after would be "gain"- even better than anything I have experienced in this life. That is an immense reassurance. But questions still lingered; questions pertaining to the timing and manner of my dying; the when and the how.

The question of timing affected me because I still had things to do, places to go, people to see. I was not afraid of death, but I was in no hurry. I had people who needed me and depended on me, particularly Esther Ruth, my wife of over 45 years, and my sons and grandchildren. It was hard for me to imagine a world (this life) that did not include me!

As I wrestled with these questions, I found my thoughts drawn to a sermon I had preached on Psalm 116. In this psalm, the writer records his experience of a life-threatening illness or event. In desperate straits, he cried out to God. And God answered! God delivered him from death. So he pours out heart-felt words of praise and thanks to God. Let's capture the sense of this beautiful psalm:

Verse 3 reads:

The snares of death encompassed me;
the pangs of Sheol laid hold on me;
I suffered distress and anguish.

The poetic language is graphic: the snares, ropes or cords of death were wrapped around him. Sheol is the Hebrew name for the place of death. The word translated "pangs" refers to anything narrow or confining and restrictive, thus causing distress. Death, with its accompanying distress was closing in on him. This was the experience the writer was reflecting on as he composed this psalm. In his distress, what did he do? Look at verse 4:

Then I called on the name of the Lord: "O Lord, I pray, deliver my soul!"

And God answered. This is clear in verses 8-9:

8 For you have delivered my soul from death, my eyes from tears, my feet from stumbling;
9 I will walk before the Lord in the land of the living.

In answer to his prayer, God saved the psalmist from death and restored him. It was a dramatic answer to prayer and a dramatic deliverance from the jaws of death. His gratitude for God's answer permeates the psalm and was the reason for his writing, as is clear in the opening verse:

^{1} I love the Lord, because he has heard my voice and my pleas for mercy.

He closes the psalm on the same note in verses 17-19.

^{17} I will offer to you the sacrifice of thanksgiving and call on the name of the Lord.
^{18} I will pay my vows to the Lord in the presence of all his people,
^{19} in the courts of the house of the Lord, in your midst, O Jerusalem. Praise the Lord!

At first glance, this psalm may seem a strange place to go to find reassurance in my illness and as I contemplated my own mortality. Yes, by hindsight now I can certainly echo the psalmist's words of praise as I review the two years since my diagnosis: the success of my cancer treatment and my ongoing remission. The Lord has heard my prayers and I am still "walking before the Lord in the land of the living." Praise the Lord! But at the time of my hospitalization I had no such reassurance. Even now, the threat of the cancer's recurrence and my own impending mortality still hang over my head. What comfort did I find in this Psalm?

I face an additional dilemma. I keep a prayer list or prayer journal. I find it encouraging to look back over my prayer journal from time to time and see how many check marks there are for answered prayers. But there are other entries in my prayer journal. They are names; names of people in the church, people I cared about who suffered from life threatening illnesses. They are names that I have now crossed off my list. I didn't cross them off the list because they recovered or were healed. I crossed them off because they died. I am reminded of one woman in particular. She was a faithful church member and a part of our church board. She and her husband retired and moved away from Abu Dhabi. Shortly afterwards we received word that she had been diagnosed with Multiple Myeloma; the same kind of cancer I now have. We prayed for her and followed the reports as she pursued the same regimen of treatments I would later follow. All seemed to be going well, and then we heard that the cancer had returned. Within a very short time we received the news that she had died. I crossed her name off my prayer list. What comfort might this psalm of praise for answered prayer offer to her grieving family and friends?

Embedded in Psalm 116 is a verse that I have found to be of great comfort. In many ways, it doesn't seem to fit the rest of the psalm. It is a reflection on death; particularly the death of believers, of God worshippers. As I said, in some ways it doesn't seem to fit, but in other ways it is a perfect fit. In the midst of his rejoicing and gratitude for his deliverance from death, the psalmist takes time to reflect on death from God's perspective and draw lessons on how God views death.

This is what he says in verse 15:

Precious in the sight of the Lord is the death of his saints.

What is this saying? Why is it here? What is the lesson the psalmist learned and is attempting to pass on to us?

Let me quickly dispense with one possible misunderstanding. The word "saints" is never used in Scripture to refer to some special category of spiritual heroes or elite Christians. When it is used it consistently refers to all who "worship God in spirit and truth" and follow him by faith.

This verse, then, expresses the attitude and the perspective of God on death – specifically the death of believers, his own "holy ones" or saints, his faithful ones.

Precious in the sight of the Lord is the death of his saints.

Does that sound strange to you? To understand what the psalmist is saying, we need to first take a closer look at the word "precious." Here are four synonyms I found in my Hebrew dictionary: "precious, rare, splendid, weighty." I especially like that fourth one: "Weighty" or "heavy".

I went to university in the late 1960s and early 1970s. It was a time of great social upheaval in the US and this was especially noticeable on college campuses. As in any generation,

I suppose, we created our own unique vocabulary; words that were used and overused until they took on a meaning of their own. One such word was "heavy". Any thought, idea or experience that was perceived as profound or deeply significant was described as "heavy". "That's heavy, man! That's heavy!" was heard frequently in conversations. And indeed, it was a "heavy" time in US history and on college campuses as hundreds of thousands of our age mates were drafted and sent to Vietnam, and over 50,000 never returned.

But in this word, the concept of "heavy" comes together with something that is precious or of great value. From time to time during my years in Abu Dhabi I would go to one of the jewelry stores in town to pick out a piece of gold jewelry as a gift for my wife. When I would settle on a necklace or small pendant I would ask the price. Do you know what the merchant would do? He would take it and place it on a scale and then tell me the price. The "heavier" it is, the more "precious" it is. And the more precious something is, the more attention we pay to it and the more we protect it and care for it. Costly, heavy, "precious" jewelry is kept in a locked jewelry box or even in a safe.

This is how God views the death of one of his own. It is "heavy." It is precious. It is of great significance and value. It is something that he has weighed out carefully on his scales. Here is the important point. The death of one of God's saints is never random or accidental or something that results from his being inattentive or off-duty or uncaring. The day of death for every child of God is a carefully measured and valued and weighed-out part of God's eternal plan, and it is of great significance and importance to him. In fact, the Bible tells us that the days (and length) of my life were settled in God's mind before I was ever born. As David writes in Psalm 139:16:

in your book were written, every one of them,
the days that were formed for me,
when as yet there was none of them.

This was the conclusion the psalmist came to when he was delivered from death. While he gave thanks for his deliverance this time, he also took time to reflect that his death (when it came) would not be an accident. He concluded that God had things well in hand. Nothing would or could happen to him that was outside the plan of God. This same reality is present whenever a child of God dies.

There is a small cemetery on the mission station at Kijabe, Kenya, where I grew up. On my infrequent visits back to Kijabe, I have taken the time to walk there among the graves. There are three headstones there with the name "Arensen" on them. One of them is my grandfather's. Grandpa never even visited Africa until he became too old to live on his own in the US. Then he came out to Kenya to stay with my parents. He died there two years later. The dates on his headstone reflect a long and full life. There is another headstone there for a nephew of mine – who never saw the light of day. He died of complications at birth. The third headstone is for my sister-in-law, Janis. She died at the age of 39 from a bullet wound suffered in a bandit ambush in Southern Sudan where she and my brother Lanny were serving as missionaries.

What Psalm 116:15 tells me is that not one of those deaths was an accident. Not one of them was random. Not one of them happened because God didn't care or because God was off duty. I take great comfort in that. "Precious in the sight of the Lord is the death of his saints." You see, the psalmist who wrote Psalm 116 and gave praise to God for his deliverance from death, eventually died. He didn't die that day. But he did die, on another day, on a day of God's own carefully measured and weighed out choosing.

I still don't know how or when I shall die. If I could write my own script, my cancer would remain permanently in remission and I would live to a ripe old age in good health and then die in my sleep in my own bed. But I don't get to write my own script. God has already written the script. He knows the day of my death. He knew it before I was ever born, and he has chosen the day very, very carefully. I take great confidence in that fact. I do not seek death. But at the same time, I do not fear death nor do I fret about its timing. I know that my death, as my life, is in God's hands. I wouldn't want it any other way.

Final Words

My journey continues. And so will yours. There are good days and not so good days. Walking by faith is a daily choice. It is my prayer and hope that the Scripture passages and principles I have shared in these chapters will prove to be as big a help to you as they have been to me. When the storms of life come and emotions wobble, it is essential to have solid truth to stand on; to stand on solid ground.

Before I close, I have one more thing I need to say. I have written this book with a particular audience in mind and therefore with certain presuppositions. The audience I have in mind consists of people who are already followers of Jesus Christ; individuals who have trusted in Jesus as their Savior from sin and therefore believe in the hope of eternal life that is promised in the Bible. I recognize that there may be some who read these chapters for whom this is not the case. If you are one of those people and you would like to know more about Jesus and the life he came to offer, I have a simple assignment for you. It will only take you 21 days. You can do this assignment by yourself or with another person.

Find a Bible and locate the Gospel of John. John has 21 chapters. Read one chapter a day. As you read, look for and record as many answers as you can find to the following four questions:

- Who is Jesus? (questions of identity – look for names, titles, descriptive phrases)
- Where did he come from? (the question of origin)
- Why did he come? (the question of purpose)
- How do we know? (the question of evidence)

At the end of the twenty-one days, you will face a simple (but extremely important!) question. In John 20:31, John writes:

But these are written so that you may believe that Jesus is the Christ, the Son of God, and that by believing you may have life in his name.

So here is the critical question: do you believe what you have read and the answers to the questions you have found in the text? I say that it is an important question because of the following verses, found in the first epistle of John:

> [11] And this is the testimony, that God gave us eternal life, and this life is in his Son. [12] Whoever has the Son has life; whoever does not have the Son of God does not have life. [13] I write these things to you who believe in the name of the Son of God, that you may know that you have eternal life (1 John 5:11-13).

It is only when you can answer the "belief" question in the affirmative that the assurances and promises I have expounded in this book will begin to make sense. The world we live in offers a cacophony of voices, all claiming to point the way to satisfaction, fulfillment and happiness. Jesus said, "I came that (you) may have life and have it abundantly." (John 10:10) I have staked my life (and death) on that promise and I have found it abundantly fulfilled in all the ups and downs of my journey. God's promise of abundant (and eternal) life doesn't begin when we die. It begins when we believe in Jesus as "the way, the truth and the life." (John 14:6) It can begin for you today!

Acknowledgments

Thanks to Suzi Malan for editorial suggestions and proof-reading the different stages of this work, to Shel Arensen for editorial comments and publishing advice and to all who encouraged me along the way. Most of all, thank you to the congregation of the Evangelical Community Church of Abu Dhabi who first listened so attentively to the sermons that make up the body of this work and who stood by me with such love, concern and prayers during the early days of my cancer journey.

CPSIA information can be obtained
at www.ICGtesting.com
Printed in the USA
FSHW020741030619
58670FS